# TENDING THE FIRE

## THE STORY OF MARIA MARTINEZ

# TENDINC THE FIRE

## THE STORY OF MARIA MARTINEZ

MONDO

*Worlds of love and all good things to the four traveling cousins: Chris, Doug, "Little" Juddi, and Jan.*
*And for you, too, Judson—you were aboard in spirit.*
*I would like to express my gratitude to Susan Eddy, Editorial Director at Mondo Publishing, for Maria's rebirth,*
*and thank my editor, Cynthia Levinson, for giving the book such a beautiful second coming.*

For information contact:
Mondo Publishing
980 Avenue of the Americas, New York, NY 10018
Visit our website at www.mondopub.com

Printed in China
09 10 11 12 13    9 8 7 6 5 4 3 2 1
ISBN 978-1-60201-967-6
Text originally published by Rising Moon Northland Publishers 1997
Cover and Book Design by Michelle Farinella
Artwork for Chapter Openers copyright 1997 by Stephanie Bucholz. Used by permission.

Photography Credits:
Every effort has been made to trace the ownership of copyright materials in this book and to obtain
permission for their use.

Front cover (large), page 68, and pages 102–103: Edward S. Curtis, Courtesy Palace of the Governors
(MNM/DCA), 144699; front cover (center) and page 101: Maurice Eby, Courtesy Palace
of the Governors (MNM/DCA),131843; page 11: © Charles & Josette Lenars/CORBIS; page 13: ©
Bettmann/CORBIS; page 18: Denver Public Library, Western History Collection, Wolle Estate 1977,
Z-1546; page 22: © Franz-Marc Frei/CORBIS; page 28: Francesca Yorke © Dorling Kindersley; page 34:
T. Harmon Parkhurst, Courtesy Palace of the Governors (MNM/DCA),003791; page 40: T. Harmon
Parkhurst, Courtesy Palace of the Governors (MNM/DCA),012400; page 42: Denver Public Library,
Western History Collection, H. S. Poley, P-1453; page 47: © CORBIS; page 52: Denver Public Library,
Western History Collection, Jesse L. Nusbaum, N-318; page 58: © Lake County Museum/CORBIS; page
61: "Maria Martinez Coiling Clay, ca. 1930-1960," photograph, Eldred R. Harrington Photograph
Collection (PICT 000-299-3944), Center for Southwest Research, University Libraries, University of
New Mexico; page 62: Denver Public Library, Western History Collection, Jesse L. Nusbaum, N-275;
page 66: Denver Public Library, Western History Collection, X-3027; page 74: T. Harmon Parkhurst,
Courtesy Palace of the Governors (MNM/DCA), 003797; page 76–77: Beulah Easton, Courtesy Palace
of the Governors (MNM/DCA), 200007; page 80: Jesse Nusbaum, Courtesy Palace of the Governors
(MNM/DCA), 119612; page 82: Andy Crawford © Dorling Kindersley; pages 84–85: T. Harmon
Parkhurst, Courtesy Palace of the Governors (MNM/DCA),001038; page 89: Denver Public Library,
Western History Collection, Wolle Estate 1977, Z-1545; page 91: © Bettmann/CORBIS; page 93: Julian
Martinez, 10"x6.25", Photographed by T. Harmon Parkhurst, Courtesy of Mark Sublette Medicine Man
Gallery, Tucson, AZ and Santa Fe, NM; page 97: Denver Public Library, Western History Collection,
X-30341; pages 110–111: © National Geographic/Getty Images

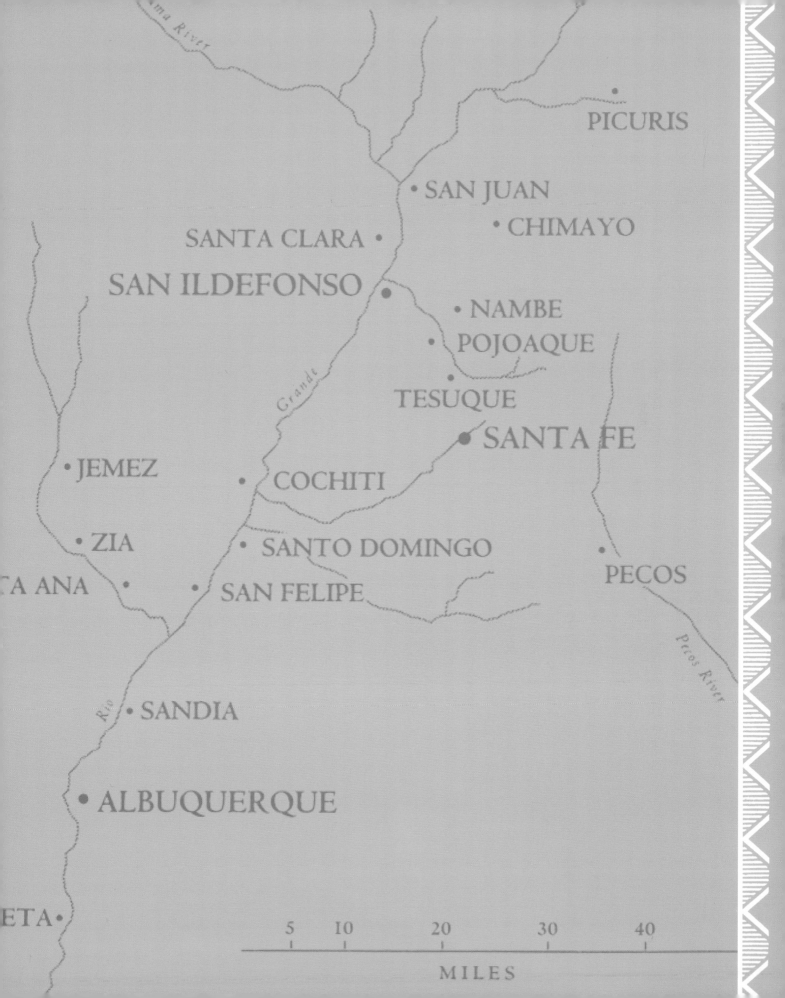

# CONTENTS

Map of the
Rio Grande
Pueblos of
New Mexico

# CHAPTER ONE

On April 5, 1887,[1] in the quiet pueblo of San Ildefonso (San il-duh-FON-soh),

New Mexico, a tiny girl was born. She was the daughter of prosperous Native

American farmer Tomas Montoya and his wife, Reyes. The couple—who had

two other daughters, Maximiliana (Anna) and Desideria—named their new

baby Maria Antonia and gave her the Tewa name Poveka, meaning Pond

Lily. Little did they realize she would one day become a renowned Native

American potter.

[1]April 5, 1887. This is recorded as Maria's birthdate on her Certificate of Baptism, which was made
in 1952 when Maria's son researched the date of her birth. Because no record was made at the time
of her birth, Maria never knew exactly how old she was.

The Montoyas belonged to the Tewa tribe, pueblo dwellers who were called "the peaceful people of the Southwest." Like their neighbors the family lived in an adobe, a house made of sun-dried bricks of clay. Situated on the Rio Grande,[2] about 25 miles from Santa Fe, San Ildefonso was an intimate little world where people sang up the corn, called down the rain, and danced together with Mother Earth. The Pueblo people were hard working. Men cultivated fields of corn, squash, beans, and cotton. The women made baskets and fine pottery.

Maria and her sisters grew up in a close-knit family. The girls' play imitated the lives of their mother, aunts, and the other women of the pueblo as they went about their daily tasks of housekeeping, childcare, pottery and basket making, gardening, and cooking.

When Maria was about 8 years old, she and Desideria built a playhouse by mortaring adobe bricks together with clay from the acequia. Once it was built, the little girls took three-legged stools to the playhouse each morning. After opening the door, they set the stools inside and laid their dolls upon them. Soft squirrel skin stuffed with straw shaped Maria's doll. Red flannel cloth patches formed its eyes and mouth.

As soon as the "babies" were asleep under their hand-woven blankets, the little girls swept the floors with soft sagebrush brooms their father had made. After changing to stiff rabbitbrush brooms, they swept the yard around the little house, or casita, just as the pueblo women did around their adobes. With this done, they took their play metates and manos and began grinding corn for tortillas. Maria and Desideria loved doing these "grown-up" lady chores.

---

[2] **Rio Grande.** A river that rises in the San Juan Mountains in southwest Colorado and flows into the Gulf of Mexico. Means "Big River" in Spanish.

*San Ildefonso is one of 18 Rio Grande pueblos. The Tewa name for the village is "Powhoge," which means "where the water cuts through." Once strictly a farming community, it is now a thriving center of artistic activity, largely due to the work of Maria Martinez.*

In the spring and summer, the sisters ate lunch in the playhouse and were always allowed to ask friends to join them. Maria loved eating there but began longing for dishes that would not have to be returned to the big house each evening. After all, didn't every grown-up house have dishes? She and Desideria decided to make their own cups, bowls, and plates.

The next day they walked to the acequia and dug clay. After hauling it to the yard in front of the playhouse, they sat down in the sunshine to make pottery dishes. The finished bowls looked good, but the next day, after drying, they cracked.

Maria wondered how it could be possible that the same clay used for walls of houses could crack when used to make dishes. The girls decided to ask their Tia Nicolasa.

They crossed the plaza to her house where they found their aunt making yeast bowls in the shady yard. Maria told her about their dishes cracking. Nicolasa nodded her head; she understood what had happened and suggested they watch as she worked the clay for a few minutes.

The girls sat quietly and observed as Tia Nicolasa, who had learned pottery making from her mother, began forming a bowl from the damp clay. She was one of the finest potters in the pueblo and worked quickly. First, she used a puki to pat out a flat, round base for the bottom of the vessel. Then she began rolling coils which she added to the base. The girls noted how carefully she attached coil after coil to build the sides of the bowl.

Later, as they were eating lunch, Maria told her aunt that she thought she'd learned why their dishes had cracked. Could it be because they hadn't begun with a tortilla shape for the bottom as Nicolasa did? The girls had simply rolled coils into a base, which cracked from the strain when it dried. Their aunt agreed that they should have started with a flat piece of clay as she had done.

*Native American women from many Southwest pueblos made pottery. Pueblo dwellers still make pottery today.*

After lunch the three returned to the shady side of the house where the four yeast bowls waited, covered with an old sheet. Nicolasa advised the girls to make pottery in the shade, explaining that the sun dried the clay too quickly, causing it to crack. Then she asked each girl to form a pot. They patted out the base until it was smooth and flat, then tried to imitate their aunt as she spun the coils between her palms to form the sides of the bowl. She showed them how to make the rolls long enough to go around the edge of the base. They learned to fit each row neatly, joining the ends firmly, building row upon row. The older woman emphasized the importance of turning the pot so that the coils would not be joined in the same place each time and grow higher there. When the bowls were deep enough, Nicolasa instructed the girls to wet their fingers and flatten the rolls until the sides were uniformly smooth inside and out. Following this step, they used a stone to burnish each piece until it was silky-smooth.

After the bowls were finished, Maria and Desideria thanked their aunt for the lesson. Nicolasa told them to remember two important things as they grew up: always share their pottery knowledge and help the women of the pueblo in any way they could. The little girls solemnly promised to do as she suggested. They carefully placed the bowls in their shawls and trotted home, eager to begin using their dishes.

Desideria and Anna liked to make pottery, but they were not as interested in working with clay as Maria was. She loved forming pots and practiced the whole summer, making simple, straight-sided bowls. Soon her work improved, and one morning she tried a more difficult shape—a jar with a long neck and a bulging belly. Patiently she built coil upon coil. At the top of the vessel, she made each row smaller to form a neck. When she was finished, her parents said it was a well-turned piece and suggested she show it to Tia Nicolasa.

Her aunt threw up her graceful hands in delight, taking the jar and turning it round and round in admiration. "Yes, my niece will be a fine potter when she grows up," Nicolasa murmured, "but she must continue to practice."

The next time she fired her own pottery, Maria's aunt promised to put the new jar in with her own pieces. Maria could even help with the firing if she liked. Walking home, the little girl began to count the days until they fired the ware.

Soon Nicolasa had enough pieces ready for a firing. She sent word to Maria that they would begin early the next morning before the wind came up as all was still. That night the young potter could hardly sleep. It was a great honor to fire pottery with her aunt, but she felt worried. What if her jar cracked? Or worse, what if her jar exploded all over the other pots and ruined them? Just the thought of that made her shudder.

# CHAPTER TWO

The next morning, just before dawn, Nicolasa and Maria built a fire in a

shallow pit behind the house. First they spread pieces of broken pottery for

a base, then stacked their new pots on top of it. After covering the ware with

more broken pot shards, they piled on cedar logs and sprinkled cornmeal

on the heap to bless the firing. Nicolasa said a prayer and touched a match

to the cedar-bark kindling.

A blaze sprang up. Each time it flickered or nearly died, they laid on more wood. After several hours of intense heat, the fire was allowed to burn out. Now they must wait for the pottery to cool; they didn't want the cold air to strike the hot pieces, which would cause them to crack when uncovered.

Hours later when the pots were unearthed, Maria's jar looked beautiful—no cracks or smudges. It was such a fine piece that the little girl gave it to her mother. Again, Nicolasa encouraged Maria to continue practicing so that she would become a fine potter, one who could share her knowledge with the other Pueblo women of her generation. Reyes was proud of the jar and set it in a niche above the fireplace for all to admire. She and Tomas both urged Maria to keep trying more difficult pottery shapes. Each form presented another challenge, and sometimes Maria felt that every time she made a different-shaped vessel, it was like starting all over again. She was glad she lived near Tia Nicolasa; her aunt was always willing to help and had many hints that she shared with her niece.

The summer went quickly and fall came to the pueblo. Maria put away her sacks of clay and tools because she knew she would have little time for pottery making after school began.

The pueblo school started in September. Maria enjoyed studying and brought home good grades. She liked her new teacher, Miss Grimes, who was young and pretty, but had the snow-white hair of an older woman. It was rumored that her hair turned white overnight, and the children often speculated about what terrible thing could happen to change the color of a person's hair. Miss Grimes was a good teacher, and she was also gentle and kind. Maria loved to spend time with her after school, helping to dust erasers and clean the blackboard.

During the school term, Miss Grimes visited the homes of all her pupils in the pueblo. She enjoyed calling on the Montoya family and often

*Maria's aunt taught her how to build a kiln for firing pottery. Here, Maria stacks chips of cow dung over her pots for firing.*

told Reyes and Tomas what fine daughters they had. If Miss Grimes happened to be at anyone's house at mealtime, she always sat down and ate with the family and then helped clear the table and wash the dishes. The Pueblo people appreciated her friendly ways, and most of the pupils studied hard to please her.

As fall passed, the golden leaves of the cottonwood trees fell, drifting against the fences and floating down the clear water of the acequia. Winter came. Snow sifted to the ground and settled on the soft, ocher edges of the adobe houses that snuggled down into it.

One thing Maria liked best about wintertime was storytelling. After the farm work was finished and the fruit and vegetables were stored, her family sat by the fire and spun tales of long ago. It was part of their heritage to do so. The stories on those long winter evenings were usually about birds and animals. As the tale developed, there were songs to be sung, and each story ended with a lesson for the children. In this way Tewa customs were not lost to later generations.

An elderly couple, Jaime and Marta, were the best storytellers in the pueblo. Following the first snowfall, Reyes told the girls to ask the old people to come visit that evening. Excitedly, Maria and Desideria raced down the hill to the house at the bottom of the slope and knocked on the door. When the elderly man appeared, and the girls asked them to come visit, he answered just as always, "I'd like to go, but my wife's old and cranky, so maybe she won't let me."

And old Marta, when she heard him, pressed her lips together as she always did. Then she blew her breath through her lips and said, "He's so old himself he may not be able to walk up the hill, but I'll help him all I can."

Then the old people laughed, and Jaime said, "We will be very happy to come. Please tell your mother so."

After the dishes were done, the family sat before the fire. Maria could hardly wait for their visitors to arrive. Finally she saw their torches flickering outside. When the couple came into the room, greeting everyone and stamping the snow from their feet, Jaime handed their pine-splinter torches to the girls' father. Tomas knocked the flames into the fireplace and laid the sticks on the hearth, where his guests could get them for the return trip. Maria loved the coziness of the room on those nights. When everyone was seated comfortably around the blazing fire, she was completely happy and wished the night would last forever.

The stories began. Jaime started the first one, and when he was through, he usually chose the girls' father to tell the next. When Tomas's story was finished, he pointed to someone else, and that person started a tale.

After several more stories, Reyes and Anna bustled into the kitchen and brought back bowls of popcorn and plates of biscochitos (cookies), hot chocolate for the girls, and a pot of coffee for the grown-ups. Tomas went to the outside storehouse and brought in a treat he had saved since summer: a large watermelon. He was proud of the melons he grew and knew that his visitors considered them a special treat. They always saved the seeds in their handkerchiefs to take home and plant the next spring.

When they had eaten the last cookie crumb, the stories began again. They continued until the children were sleepy, which always signaled Jaime and Marta to say they must go. The old people lit their torches in the fireplace, and Tomas went down the hill to see them home. Reyes and the girls stood in the doorway until the wavering lights disappeared down the trail and around the bend.

Maria went to bed. In a few minutes Tomas was back, and the little girl could hear her parents murmuring comfortably in their bedroom. Before long they were all in their beds, tucked under warm homespun blankets, and sleeping soundly.

Maria's parents were loving and kind, and her childhood peaceful and happy in that quiet New Mexico pueblo of San Ildefonso.

# CHAPTER THREE

When Maria was 10 years old, the dreaded "spotted sickness", smallpox,

struck the pueblo, and several people died. Maria contracted it. She burned

with a high temperature for days and nearly died. After the fever had passed

and Maria lay watching the snow settle on the branches outside her window,

she recalled that her mother kept telling her something during the days

when she was so ill. What, she could not remember.

When she was strong enough to talk, the little girl asked her mother about it. Reyes said that during the worst of the illness, she and Tomas had promised God they would take Maria on a pilgrimage across the mountains to El Santuario de Chimayo (Chee-my-OH) if her life was spared. They would go when she was strong again, her mother said. Maria lay dreamily thinking about making a pilgrimage. She felt important—even Anna, her older sister, had never done such a thing.

*El Santuario de Chimayo (The Sanctuary of Chimayo), New Mexico, is visited by thousands of pilgrims each year. Because the earth there is said to have healing powers, the sanctuary is considered one of the truly holy places in North America. It is about 12 miles from San Ildefonso.*

Spring came, lambs were born, robins returned to find worms, and Tomas and Anna started a garden. In early June, Reyes told Maria that in four days the little girl and her father would start the pilgrimage to Chimayo. Maria wanted to know if her mother would be going. Since she was expecting a baby, Reyes could not walk so far. Father and daughter would go together, but Reyes and one of Maria's aunts would meet them at the church with the wagon so the family could ride home. The little girl looked forward to having so much time alone with her busy father.

Reyes awakened Maria that pilgrimage morning while the sky was still dark. Tomas was already in the kitchen eating breakfast by lamplight. After the little girl had eaten tortillas and a piece of her mother's homemade cheese and had drunk a cup of milk with a little hot coffee spooned into it, she put on her best purple dress and the special high, white moccasins that were usually saved for Mass and ceremonial dances. Her mother braided Maria's long hair and pinned it at the back of her neck, then handed her a beaded rosario.

Before the sun rose over Black Mesa[3] (MAY-sa), the pilgrims set out carrying a small basket of food and a pottery olla of water. In the shadow of the great, dark mesa that hovered over the land, father and daughter followed a trail uphill and down, walking along dry creek beds, crossing arroyos, and picking their way over large rocks. After reaching level ground, they walked without speaking, fingering their rosaries and praying.

Tomas stopped often so Maria would not get too tired. At noon they ate lunch in the cool shade of a spreading cottonwood tree on the bank of the river. After the short rest, they started again. It grew hot, and they walked more slowly. Maria was beginning to tire. Her father watched her

[3] **Black Mesa.** A mesa is a small flat-topped hill with two or more steep, usually perpendicular sides. "Black Mesa" is just north of San Ildefonso. It was home to the people of San Ildefonso for nine months in 1694, when the Spaniards were fighting them for control over the region.

closely, but she stumbled on. They rested often now. Late in the afternoon, father and daughter struggled into the tiny village of Chimayo.

The Santuario stood at the end of the street. When they reached the humble little building, Maria saw her mother and aunt waiting in the wagon. How glad she was to see them! The two women climbed down to join them, and the family strolled under the great arching cottonwood trees into the cool, dark sanctuary saying their rosarios. As they entered the church, Maria and the two women covered their heads with their shawls, and all four of them knelt in prayer and made the sign of the cross. Maria felt calm, but she wondered what the ceremony would be like.

In front of the altar, flickering candlelight outlined the figures of the saints. The priest came forward and directed Maria to a door at the left of the altar. Her mother spoke to the padre about what her daughter should do. When the two finished their hushed conversation, Reyes handed Maria a holy medal. She told her daughter to go through the door and down four steps to a tiny room with an earthen floor. There she must scrape up a small amount of soil with the medal and rub herself with what her church felt was holy earth. When she was through, she was to recite the Lord's Prayer and then fill the water bottle with more of the same earth to take home. Back at San Ildefonso, Maria would mix the holy earth with water and drink it before breakfast the next four days. Her people believed that this would keep her in good health for the rest of her life.

Maria did as she was told. Afterwards, when she came back into the sanctuary carrying the filled bottle, her mother was waiting for her. Reyes took the bottle and handed the young pilgrim a bundle to lay on the altar as an offering of gratitude that her life was spared. In it was a length of purple velvet, a delicate rosary, a soft piece of buckskin, and three ten-cent pieces.

After leaving her bundle at the feet of the carved Santo Niño, Maria rejoined her kneeling mother, father, and aunt. Together the family left the church and walked out into a blazing sunset of red, purple, and pink. Maria was exhausted, but she felt strangely peaceful.

The trip home went more quickly, since they were riding in the wagon. The horses were rested and fresh for the return trip. Maria was so tired that she curled up in the back on a pallet of blankets and didn't wake until Tomas picked her up and gently put her down on her bed.

Maria never forgot this spiritual pilgrimage to Chimayo. She spoke with wonderment of the journey frequently during her lifetime and felt the experience deeply affected both her spiritual life and work experience. She always held a special place in her heart for the beautiful little church in Chimayo.

Back at the pueblo, Maria went to tell her great-grandmother about the pilgrimage. She and her sisters enjoyed visiting the ancient lady, who lived with their grandmother at the west end of the village. They especially liked the two-story adobe in which the two older women lived. The dwelling was in good condition, but it was very old. The house had belonged to Old Grandmother's father when he was governor of the pueblo long, long ago. The girls were fascinated by the hatchways in the ceilings of the first floor where ladders had once stretched high into the upper rooms. Old Grandmother said the ladders were used to move from level to level in case the Navajos or Apaches attacked the pueblo in those early, more turbulent times.

Now that their great-grandmother was very old, she who had been tall and broad-shouldered had shrunk to the size of the two younger girls. People still spoke of what a strong woman she used to be and told stories of how she could dance better, grind more corn, and care for a larger garden than any other woman in San Ildefonso. Though she was frail and weak, her hair was wavy and thick, and Maria loved to comb and brush it, making fat braids, which she wrapped around the still proud head in great silver coils.

When she was not too tired, Old Grandmother, in an aged voice that twittered like a bird, told them stories of past days. Sometimes the tiny woman even played with the girls or made clothes for their dolls. But more and more often, she lay on her bed and gazed out the door at the fields of corn and the sheep grazing in their peaceful pastures. When she was like that, Maria's grandmother said the "old one" was dreaming of the days when she was young.

One day Old Grandmother sent word for the family to come. As they gathered around her bedside, she told them she didn't have long to live. She had already given away most of her possessions, she reminded them. The big house would be Grandmother's, of course. Her dance costumes with matching jewelry she wished her great-granddaughters to share. That left only her pottery to divide, and she wanted the girls to have most of that as well.

When the apricot and peach trees began to bloom, the old one died. Soon after the funeral, Grandmother asked the women of the family to come to the house. It was time for the great-granddaughters to choose their pottery, but first they must open a door that led to a secret storeroom where the pots were kept.

Most pueblo houses had rooms off the kitchen where supplies were stored. Reyes often sent one of her daughters into her own storeroom to get items she needed for cooking. They knew all about these rooms, but Old Grandmother's was different. Instead of having a hinged door that swung back and forth, this old house had a storeroom with a tiny portal that fit tightly into the opening and which had to be lifted in and out of the wall.

As they worked at the opening, Grandmother said she thought the small entrance had been built that way to protect supplies from intruders. The kitchen had been remodeled some years ago, so the old room with the tiny door had not been opened in a long time.

They stopped to eat at noon. After a short rest, they went back to work. Maria took the last turn chipping at the door. She felt a shiver of excitement at the thought of seeing the old pottery. When she had freed all but one corner, she called Tia Nicolasa so she could be the first to glimpse Old Grandmother's collection.

When the portal was finally lifted out and the shelves of pottery were revealed, the women were amazed. There were so many shapes and sizes! Most were larger than they were used to seeing. They identified pots from San Juan Pueblo and others made by the women of Santa Clara. There were decorated pots and plain pots, dark red pots that were the color of polished leather, pots that were brown and squatty, and even a pot made by the Apaches.

Anna chose one that would be useful in the new house to which she and her fiancé would be moving when they were married. Maria chose a dark red one made by her tribe, the Tewa. When Grandmother asked what she was going to do with it, Maria replied, "Put it in the storehouse at home and fill it with popcorn. Then we'll have it ready for winter."

"I'm going to put blue corn in mine," said Desideria.

"Well," said Tia Nicolasa, "those are both good jars that you have there. If you keep them filled with corn and use them right, they will last in your time as long as they have already. That's the good thing about pottery. If you use it right, it helps you right."

That was another unforgettable day for Maria. The sight of so many fine pots was an inspiration to her. Someday she hoped to make pottery as beautiful as that in Old Grandmother's storeroom. She resolved to spend even more time working with Tia Nicolasa learning to make different shapes. As her aunt always said, "In pottery the old saying of 'practice makes perfect' is right." Maria knew that she had not spent much time "making perfect" the last few months, because her father had asked Maria

*Pictured is a large hand-crafted pot from Santa Clara Pueblo.*
*Santa Clara is about 10 miles from San Ildefonso.*

and Desideria to spend more time helping their pregnant mother while he was away at the fields.

When Reyes and Tomas were newly married, they had very little land, and the acreage Tomas cultivated was near the pueblo. As time passed, he prospered, for he was a good farmer. Tomas gradually acquired more land, much of it away from San Ildefonso. Taking care of the crops kept him far from the pueblo most weekdays. He always came home Saturday and Sunday to be with the family and to go to Mass, but that was all he could manage. They were sad to be apart so much of the time.

There would be time for pottery making later. For even at this early age, Maria knew that the ancient craft of her ancestors was too much a part of her life to give up, ever.

# CHAPTER FOUR

When Maria was nearly 11 years old, her sister Juanita was born. Now that

Juanita had come into the world, Tomas told Maria and Desideria it was

doubly important that they continue to help their mother, since there was

so much to do when he was away at the other farms.

One Sunday when he was home, Tomas worked out a plan that

would give the family more time together. He said that he'd decided to plant

corn and alfalfa in the big fields that were far from the pueblo. Then he surprised them by saying that he would build a summerhouse on that land, so that Reyes and the girls could be with him. They would close the pueblo home during the summer growing season, except for the weekends when they returned for Mass. This was wonderful news to the Montoya girls, for they were a family that enjoyed one another's company.

"That all sounds good," said Mother. "The girls are old enough to help with everything, and it will be fun for me to live in the summer house where I don't have as much housework to do as here."

"That's what I thought," replied Father. "We'll all go over in the wagon after Mass tomorrow and choose a place to build the house."

After church that Sunday, the family hurried home across the plaza to make breakfast and pack a picnic lunch for the trip to choose a location. Reyes and Maria put fresh, oven-baked bread, frijoles (free-HO-les)—beans, dried meat, and ollas of water and milk into a basket.

Anna, who loved to work with animals and plants, went to the barn to help Tomas harness the team of horses. They hooked the leather traces to the wagon, then checked the reins and lines. After the team was in place, Anna stowed extra feed for the animals in the back of the wagon and drove to the house. Everybody climbed in, excited to be on their way.

They rolled down the road beside the river where the trees were big and shady. The horses were in high spirits. They trotted along with their hooves clopping on the hard road.

Up and down the hills they went, Black Mesa growing more distant every minute. Finally the lively team settled down and covered the ground at a steady pace. After several miles the valley widened. Tomas drove across a creek where two young cottonwood trees were growing side by side. They were on Montoya land now.

Tomas called "whoaaaa" to the horses, and the girls jumped out of the wagon. After helping unpack the lunch and the blankets they would sit on, Maria and Desideria rushed off to explore the countryside. After a few minutes, their mother called them to lunch.

As they ate, Reyes studied the landscape, craning her neck to see the clear water in the creek, her gaze finally settling on the surrounding shade trees. "This would be the perfect place for the house," she told Tomas.

"Yes, under the trees would be a fine place," Tomas agreed. There was plenty of fresh water and shade, and it was handy to the nearby road. Even the two young cottonwoods, quick-growing trees, would soon make extra shelter for the house. With a stick Tomas marked squares on the ground for rooms and walls. He explained to the girls, who followed him, that this would not be an adobe house like the ones in the pueblo, but one built of cedar and willow posts. Maria thought it sounded like a family playhouse and could hardly wait for it to be finished. The family decided to call the new house "Little Trees" because of the baby cottonwoods.

In the late afternoon, they packed up the remains of the picnic, piled the blankets into the wagon, hitched up the horses once more, and headed home to San Ildefonso. The next day Tomas and his helpers would return to Little Trees to start construction on the house. The family decided to move as soon as school was out, provided the house was ready by then.

The next day the girls went back to school. Anna begged to go back to Little Trees with her father to plant corn and help build the house, but her parents said she must stay in school. All three girls had a hard time concentrating on their studies because they were always thinking of the new house and all the fun they would have there.

Tomas and his workers returned to Little Trees before sunup that morning. They began construction on the casita, placing cedar posts at four corners and willow poles in the ground between them. They fastened the willows together by weaving more willow poles along the sides. They covered the woven poles with cottonwood branches, lapping them over each other so the rain could not get in. The willows along the sides were tall enough to reach the solid roofline. Tomas built the roof especially strong so the family could sleep there in the treetops during the hot nights of summer. When the simple new dwelling was finished, Tomas had even built a round outdoor oven for baking bread.

It seemed to Maria that it took a long time to finish the house at Little Trees, but Reyes thought the work went quickly. Soon the girls were helping her pack food supplies and the other items she had placed on a list. They moved beds and bedding, Juanita's cradle, cooking pots, dishes, and the metate. Desideria and Maria prepared their dolls for the trip.

Finally the long stretch of school ended. On moving day the wagon made two trips to the summerhouse with necessary things. During the second trip, there was no place for the children to sit except on top of the blankets covering the load. After what seemed like hours to Maria, they were finally there.

The walls of willow branches and the surrounding cottonwood trees made the place cozy. Reyes and the girls told Tomas what a wonderful job he had done on the house. He was pleased that his wife and daughters approved, for he and his men had worked long hours after the farming chores were done to build the casita.

When they entered the house, Tomas asked Reyes if he had placed the furniture she had sent the week before in the right places. "Oh, yes," she told him in her pleasant way, "everything is just fine."

When he left the house to unharness the horses and feed them grain, Reyes giggled and told the girls that every single thing was put in the wrong place! "We mustn't tell father, though, for he tried very hard to make everything nice," Reyes insisted, still chuckling. The backward furniture arrangement would be their secret, and they would change things as needed.

*Maria (left) was always close with her sisters.*
*Here she stands with her older sister, Anna.*

Maria never forgot how Reyes and Tomas always tried to please each other and how careful they were not to hurt each other's feelings.

And so the wonderful summer began. The family was to spend many happy hours in this "tree house." All her life Maria talked of that time, remembering the days before Anna got married when they were all together in that leafy shelter by the flowing stream. She spoke of going to bed on the roof, of falling asleep with a million twinkling stars above, and of awakening in the chilly light of dawn to pull a blanket up around her shoulders, safe and happy to be with her mother, father, and sisters in the best of all places, Little Trees.

# CHAPTER FIVE

Maria enjoyed attending the pueblo school and expected to finish her

studies there. To her surprise, though, after three years' attendance,

Maria and Desideria were chosen by the governor of San Ildefonso

to attend St. Catherine's School in Santa Fe for two years.

Reyes had attended St. Catherine's as a girl, so she knew what her

daughters would need at the big school in Santa Fe. She began sewing new

clothes for them. In the pueblo they had always dressed as the other women and girls—in flowered or striped blouses and plain dresses that fastened over one shoulder and under the other arm. They wore warm moccasins in the winter and went barefoot in the summertime. Their long hair was tied at the back of the neck with colorful hand-woven cloth strips. But Reyes felt (as did many Native Americans of that time) that it would be better if Maria and Desideria dressed as the Anglo girls did at the Santa Fe school.

That summer passed quickly. Maria used up all the clay she had making pots; she knew there would be no pottery making in Santa Fe. In the fall their parents took the nervous but excited girls to school. They wore new dresses and sat on the wagon seats instead of plopping down in the back as they usually did. They wanted to look especially nice when they arrived. It was nightfall by the time they crested the last steep hill and gazed at the glitter of the town in the valley below. The lights, shining through piñon and juniper trees, seemed very bright compared to the dark pueblo.

Living in Santa Fe and attending the large school was a great change for the Montoya girls. They were used to the freedom of the pueblo, and they found living in a dormitory difficult at first. Gradually they became used to it and made friends.

Classes at St. Catherine's were more challenging than those at the pueblo school. Most of the Catholic sisters were strict and didn't encourage laughter in the classroom. But one teacher was different. Sister Brigita, the home economics teacher, encouraged her pupils to talk. She even laughed quietly with them as they sewed, cooked, or studied about healthy foods. The Sister told Maria that she was "good with her hands." The homesick little girl was so pleased that she wrote her mother about the compliment Sister Brigita had given her.

But, oh, that letter writing! Maria did not like to write letters, although she knew she must, since her parents were eager to hear from their daughters. Desideria, who won honors in English composition at St. Catherine's, enjoyed composing a letter to her parents once a week, but for Maria it was a tiresome chore. She could think of lots of things to tell her mother and father until she sat down to write, and then her mind went blank.

The girls worked out a compromise. Desideria, who hated to sew and always had clothes to be mended, would write Maria's letters. In return, Maria, the sewing whiz, would keep her sister's mending done. After Desideria finished her writing chore, Maria copied the letter in her own handwriting and mailed it to San Ildefonso. Before the school years were over, though, Desideria was having a hard time thinking of enough news for both their letters!

In two years they returned to the pueblo. The day she arrived home, Maria hurried to see Miss Grimes. She had much to tell her about Santa Fe. Miss Grimes felt Maria would be a wonderful teacher and urged the teenaged girl to attend an eastern college in a year or two, but Maria told Miss Grimes that she wanted to stay at home. She had missed her parents, village life, and pottery making while she was away. Maria also confessed that she had nearly forgotten how to form pots while she was gone. Miss Grimes reassured her that the skill would return with practice.

With her parents' permission, the two decided that Maria should help with the pueblo school. She would sweep and clean the schoolroom each day, and in return Miss Grimes would tutor her in higher studies. There would still be ample time for making pottery.

Later that summer Maria helped Miss Grimes get ready for the opening day of school. They scrubbed the floors and whitewashed the walls, cleaned the blackboards, and cut pictures from magazines to decorate the big room. Maria checked in the new textbooks and dusted and washed the erasers. Those erasers had never been so clean!

When everything was clean, neat, and organized—when even the windows sparkled—the teacher handed Maria her own schoolbooks. The student was happy Miss Grimes was going to tutor her, but when she looked at the books that night, they appeared to be difficult. She realized that she would have to spend a lot of time studying.

That winter the two were busy as beavers keeping the school in order. Their most difficult job was chopping wood for the big potbellied stove. That stove was impossible, Maria thought, cramming it with logs. It just gobbled wood. There was no way the two women could chop enough to feed it. Finally they decided to hire a man to do the job.

When Tomas came home that night, Maria told her father their problem. Did he know anyone who could help them? He thought a minute and then said, "Julian Martinez might. His family doesn't farm much. The father makes flour sifters and saddles, and Julian helps him sometimes, but that's about all. Why doesn't Miss Grimes get Julian?"

Maria told her the next day. The teacher sent word to Julian, and a few days later the tall, handsome young man appeared. Maria would never forget turning around from cleaning the blackboard to see Julian standing there so straight and quiet.

The two young people began spending a lot of time together. Every day after school, Julian came to cut wood. Maria did her work—sweeping the classroom, cleaning the blackboards and erasers, or tidying the big room. They talked as Maria did the chores, and, always too soon, it was time for her to go home. Maria was always surprised how quickly the moments passed when they were together. Each day Julian walked home with her and hurried back to school to chop the stove wood. He enjoyed Maria's company so much, he came every day, and the woodpile grew taller and taller. That stove had never had so much wood to consume!

One day Julian proposed to her. Maria flushed and told him she

*Maria's husband, Julian.*
*Julian's Tewa name was*
*Pancano, which means*
*"The Coming of the Spirits."*

wasn't sure, since another young man wanted to marry her. Julian asked her if she loved that person. She said that she didn't, but her family thought he would be a good husband. He owned land and was a successful farmer.

Julian was quiet but didn't think that was a very good reason to get married. He would give her more time, he decided. After all, she was only 17 years old.

Maria still had not made up her mind by the next year when one day Julian came to the school with exciting news. His uncle, who was a splendid singer and played the drums for many pueblos on their feast days, had been asked by the Indian Agency to attend the 1904 St. Louis World's Fair and to bring several other Tewas with him. They would be there for four or five months, demonstrating their dances, songs, and crafts. Food and lodging on the fairgrounds would be furnished. Their traveling expenses were to be paid, and each Tewa would earn 50 dollars a month while there. It was a wonderful opportunity for those who would go, and Julian felt lucky to have been chosen as a participant.

When he told Maria that he was going, her heart fell. The thought of not seeing him for several months made her want to cry. Before she had time to be sad, though, Julian again asked for Maria's hand in marriage so that she could go away with him. She realized she loved him and could never marry another man. Julian was overjoyed, but he said it would have to be a short engagement since they must leave for St. Louis in four months.

A few evenings later, Julian and his parents came visiting, dressed in their best clothes. After they were seated, Julian's mother said to Reyes, "We have brought a gift from our son to your daughter. Here it is."

Reyes took the gift wrapped in a silk handkerchief for Maria. She thanked Mrs. Martinez and handed Julian's mother a small package for her son. Both mothers unwrapped the packages and admired the contents—rosarios strung by the young couple's mothers. These were gifts that couples of the Tewa tribe tradionally exchanged before getting married. The rosario Reyes fashioned for Julian was of blue and white beads interspersed with a few large flowered ones and featured an antique silver cross in the center. Mrs. Martinez hung Julian's necklace around Maria's neck, and Reyes slipped Maria's gift over Julian's head.

Now it was time for the fathers' part of the ceremony. Tomas asked the two young people to kneel before him. Placing a hand on each dark head, he prayed that their life together be good and happy. Julian's father did the same, as did their mothers.

After this Tewa prayer ceremony, Mrs. Martinez gave Maria a bundle she had brought with her. "We have brought the bride's clothes," she said. "We want you to be our daughter soon."

*Maria dressed in clothing similar to that she would have worn on her wedding day.*

The bride's manta—a straight, sleeveless dress, caught on one shoulder—was a beautiful midnight blue, with a flowered blouse to wear under it. The upper parts of the blouse sleeves were made of blue silk; the lower parts and the ruffles at the wrists were pink. There was a pink scarf for Maria's head and an orange shawl embroidered with many-colored flowers, imported from Europe. Maria loved the colorful wedding garments and thanked the Martinez family.

The best part of the outfit, Maria thought, was the moccasins. They were beautifully crafted, with black soles that turned up around the edges. The upper parts were of white, tanned deer hide and wrapped smoothly round and round her legs. Maria's moccasins had always been nice, but she had never owned any as fine as these.

Before the Martinez family left that night, Tomas told Maria that he was giving her the house that had belonged to his mother. Maria was thrilled. She had always loved the small adobe. There she would make her pottery and live with the person she loved best in the world: her husband, Julian.

# CHAPTER SIX

For the next week, Maria and her mother and sisters were busy preparing

for the wedding. They scrubbed the house from floor to ceiling and white-

washed the walls. Reyes made tamales, frijoles, meat stew, and roasted

cabrito (goat meat). They  baked loaves of crusty golden bread in the round

outdoor oven and mixed up Reyes' little sweet cakes. No matter how busy

they were, every night before bedtime, Reyes rubbed Maria's hands with

tallow (animal fat), so they would be soft and pretty for the wedding.

During that time many friends came to the house, bringing gifts for the young couple. Maria's favorite was a double-spouted wedding jar that Tia Nicolasa had made. It was cream-colored, with good luck symbols of flowers and water snakes painted on it in red and black. Nobody made better pottery than her aunt, Maria thought.

Finally everything was ready. Saturday morning dawned, and the wide New Mexico sky was blue and clear. The Tewa part of Maria and Julian's wedding ceremony would be held before the Catholic wedding Mass on Sunday.

At noon the bridegroom's procession strode up the hill with Julian in the lead. Beside him walked his Uncle Juan. Julian looked splendid in a silk shirt with pink and blue sleeves and a colorful blanket. His long, black hair was in shining braids wrapped in red silk handkerchiefs. On his legs were white buckskin leggings sporting long fringes. He wore beautiful beaded moccasins.

Behind the two men walked Julian's parents. The rest of the Pueblo people followed to the Montoya's house, where Tomas opened the door. Eighty people swarmed into the house, but the crowded room grew hushed as they waited for Maria to appear.

In a moment the bedroom door opened, and the lovely young woman shyly came into the room. She looked beautiful in her bridal clothes. Maria walked slowly to Julian's parents and bowed. They bowed back—twice to the right and twice to the left—and then embraced her. Julian did the same before her mother and father. Then the young couple knelt before their parents while Reyes took the rosario from Maria's neck and placed it around Julian's. In turn, his mother gave Maria the necklace he had been wearing. The four parents put their hands gently on the heads of the young couple and blessed them.

An elderly man, the religious head of the pueblo, came forward with the double-spouted wedding jar Nicolasa had made for Maria. The holy man added a pinch of herbs to the filled water vessel, invited bride and groom to take a sip, and then he prayed. Following the prayer, he placed his hands on their heads in blessing. Next, he opened the front door, threw the rest of the water to the ground in one sparkling arc, then handed the wedding jar back to Maria.

Following the Tewa ceremony, Tomas invited everyone to stay for the tribal wedding celebration. They feasted and visited until it was time for the bridegroom and his family to go home. Tomorrow would be the wedding Mass at the church. Maria and Julian hated to say goodbye, but it would not be for long this time. They would have the rest of their lives together.

After the nuptial Mass the next day, everybody went back to the Montoyas' for more feasting, laughter, and merrymaking. Soon someone began tuning a guitar, a man picked up a fiddle, and out came a banjo. In a minute everyone was dancing to the music. Julian and Maria were having such a good time, but then they heard a knock at the door. It was the man who was taking them to catch the train to the St. Louis World's Fair.

The newlyweds barely had time to change their clothes and grab the bags they'd packed several days ago. They kissed their parents, shook hands, and waved goodbye to friends. The sounds of laughter, dancing, and singing followed the young couple as the wagon creaked out of the pueblo and down the road.

In St. Louis, President Theodore Roosevelt[4] pushed a golden button to start the fair that celebrated the area's 100 years in the Union. Gunboats in the harbor of the Mississippi River shot a stream of cannonballs, and

---

[4] **Theodore Roosevelt (1858-1919).** The 26th president of the United States, Roosevelt was perhaps best known for supporting laws aimed at conserving natural resources, and for his support of the "little man". He won the Nobel Peace Prize in 1906.

*About 20 million people from all over
the world attended the 1904 St. Louis
World's Fair. Pictured here is a part of the
large fairgrounds. Many fair goers enjoyed
displays at the automobile exhibit and
sampled a new treat, the ice cream cone,
which was first introduced at the fair.*

John Philip Sousa, the world-famous musician, composer, and marching band conductor, was a guest artist at the opening. Maria and Julian tasted an amazing new sandwich spread called peanut butter; it was first introduced at the fair that year. The exhibition stressed education and American culture and know-how.

Maria and Julian lived in special Tewa-style dwellings on the fairgrounds with the rest of the Tewas. Visitors were intrigued by the Native Americans and asked Maria and Julian many questions about their lives in the pueblo. Several times a day the Tewas presented ritual dances, which always drew large crowds. Julian did most of the talking since Maria was shy. She demonstrated pottery making, though, and sometimes she danced or drummed for the dancers. People were fascinated by the art of pottery making and watched the young woman as she made her plain, but elegant, polished bowls.

They went to the fair in the springtime, but it was late fall before they returned to the pueblo. Although they had enjoyed the time in St. Louis, they were happy to be back, especially Maria, who had been homesick the whole time she was away. Both families were waiting at the train station to meet the young married couple. Everyone was overjoyed to have Maria and Julian back again, for this had been the first time they had traveled so far away. Reyes, Tomas, and Julian's parents had worried about their children in that Midwestern city and were glad they were safely home.

Back at the pueblo, they feasted for hours. After they had eaten and rested for a bit, Julian brought out the presents he and Maria had bought for their family. They had fine lengths of dress fabric for their mothers and expensive shirts for their fathers. There were large, decorated boxes of candy for all. It was a wonderful homecoming. That night Maria went to bed happier than she had been since she left the pueblo months ago.

A few days after their return, Julian told his father-in-law that he was ready to settle down and learn to farm. Tomas was glad. He needed Julian's help, but the young man was nervous since farming was new to him.

"Maybe I won't be very good help," said Julian doubtfully. "I still don't know much about farming."

"You'll learn," Tomas assured him. "I'll teach you."

At home in the evenings, Julian told Maria about his work on the farm. He talked of how the earth looked as it fell in furrows to the sides of the plow and how tender and green the newly planted wheat looked as it peeped up from the ground. Julian saw design in everything, Maria thought.

One of the nicest things about being back in San Ildefonso was moving into their own place. The week before, Reyes and Desideria had swept and cleaned the little house until it shone as bright as one of Maria's pots. They had everything ready for Maria and Julian's arrival at the first home they would share as husband and wife.

The bride kept busy taking care of her new house. Every day her mother came to help her with housekeeping and cooking, teaching her to work at a slow and steady pace. Soon Maria caught up with these duties. She wished it wasn't wintertime and too cold and damp to make pottery; the clay would not dry properly this time of the year. Instead, on long winter days, Maria cut scraps of old dresses to make quilts. After she had the top part with the design finished, she carded wool from her father's sheep to fill it, then sewed the covers and filling together. As she stitched, she thought of the baby she was expecting in the summer and decided to make the infant a tiny quilt to match the large one. She would use some of the beautiful fabric she had bought in St. Louis to make something special for her and Julian's first child.

# CHAPTER SEVEN

Adam, their first baby, was born a few months later. He was a sturdy infant

who had a pleasant disposition and was easy to manage. From an early age,

he had a strong desire to please his parents and grandparents. Two years

later Adam welcomed a new sister, Yellow Pond Lily (from her mother's

Tewa name). Although Julian and Maria were happy about the birth of their

daughter, times were hard in the pueblo.

A long drought had destroyed the crops. When the rain finally came, it fell in torrents, flooding the fields and ruining what was left of the drought-starved corn. The raging waters washed out the acequias and broke their banks. The farms were a mess.

People were gloomy and worried, for they were running short of money with no crops to sell. Every day Tomas and Julian rushed to the farm in an attempt to salvage what they could, but it wasn't much. Maria noticed how tired and discouraged Julian looked when he came home at night. She knew how much he had come to dislike farming under the best of circumstances.

But to her surprise, one evening in 1907, Julian returned home with a smiling face. He could hardly wait to tell Maria about four men who had come from the School of American Research to visit the governor of the pueblo that day. They had been given permission to dig in the remains of an ancient village on the Pajarito Plateau (pa-ha-REE-toh pla-TOW) in Puye Canyon. The archaeologists were hiring a few men from San Ildefonso to help at the site.

Young, strong Julian, who had hoped to be chosen as a laborer, was one of the first Pueblo men hired to work with the archaeologists. Since the canyon was a long way from the village, the men would live in a camp close to the site. Julian would be away for the three summer months.

Maria helped him pack. She was sad, for this was the first time they would be separated, but she was grateful that he had a job. If Yellow Pond Lily had been older, she and the children could have gone with him. Her parents suggested that Maria close her house until Julian got back and spend the summer with them. Julian thought this was a fine idea, telling Maria he would worry less about her and the children if he knew she was staying with the Montoyas.

Saying goodbye that day was hard for Julian and Maria. Tears ran down their faces as the young woman stood by the door, holding the baby girl in her arms. Adam, standing beside her, lifted his small hand and waved goodbye to his father, who was trying hard to control his own emotions.

San Ildefonso was just too quiet that summer, Maria thought. It was so hot the children were not allowed to run and play outdoors, but stayed inside their houses, listless and pale. Women did their outside chores before the sun came up and then holed up with their children until dark. Julian and most of the young men were away working at any kind of job they could find. The older men and the women were uneasy with their absence. A feeling that something bad was going to happen filled the still air like the quiet before a storm.

*Cliff Dwellers, ancestors of the Pueblo people, had once lived on the Pajarito Plateau. The dig at Puye Canyon was one of the most famous and important archaeological studies in the Western Hemisphere. Julian Martinez worked many summers as a laborer on the digs. Here he works with other men to clean an altar in a ceremonial cave.*

The terrible heat lasted day after day. People complained that it had never been so hot. The sun baked the bare earth around the houses and burned the flowers the women had planted. Such scorching weather was especially hard on the infants of the village, and several died in one week's time. Maria tried to keep Adam and the baby cool. As she bathed and sponged Yellow Pond Lily, it seemed to the young woman that the heat was just one more oppressive part of the bad luck hovering over the pueblo.

One long, airless day, the baby became feverish. Her face was flushed, and her tiny body burned with heat. The fever seemed to come from nowhere, Maria thought. The baby girl whimpered constantly as she thrashed around her hammock cradle, unable to be still. Maria and Reyes were frightened, remembering the little ones who had died the week before. The nearest doctor was six hard hours away by wagon; the trip was hard for an adult but impossible for a sick baby.

They took turns holding Yellow Pond Lily. They tried to give her sips of cold water to drink, but she turned her head away. The baby's lips were parched and dry, burned by the high fever. Maria put her in cold baths. They gave her hot romero-weed tea to drink, but the fever would not break. They kept bathing her; she continued to cry. Maria walked the floor with her, then Reyes rocked the wailing baby, but Yellow Pond Lily still cried. Her fever continued to rise. Maria was frantic that she was unable to help her baby. Nothing seemed to work.

Finally as an exhausted Maria held her, the baby quit whimpering and seemed to grow cooler. Oh, wonder of wonders, could the fever have left her? Tears rolled down Reyes' face when she felt the little one's cold forehead. The fever was gone, yes, but Yellow Pond Lily was dead. When she saw her mother's tears, Maria understood.

That sullen gray dawn was the worst Maria had ever faced. The governor of the pueblo sent a man to the digs with the heartbreaking news that would change Julian's world.

For many months a darkness covered the world of the young parents. They tried to comfort each other and Adam, who could not understand what had happened to his sister. Their families were a loving help and so were the people of the pueblo, but the loss of Yellow Pond Lily was almost too much for the young couple. They struggled on, but they had lost a chunk of themselves that could never be replaced.

Julian had been paid for the dig with silver dollars. When Dr. Edgar Hewett, the man in charge of the expedition, brought Julian home after Yellow Pond Lily's death, he told Maria that her husband was one of his best workers and was well liked by everyone at the site. He hoped Julian would be able to work again the next summer. She nodded dully. Although it was good to hear, next summer seemed to be a lifetime away. Who knew or cared what would happen before then?

The couple shared Julian's earnings with their parents. After giving Julian some spending money, Maria put away the remainder for their expenses for the rest of the year.

# CHAPTER EICHT

That sad year finally passed. The next summer the archaeologists returned

to their dig site. A member of the expedition team came to the house to

hire Julian again. This time Julian said he would go only if Maria and Adam

could come, too. The couple had decided that the cool mountain

air would be good for their little boy. Besides, they did not want to be apart

all summer.

As the man sat in the kitchen talking to Julian and watching Maria shape a clay pot, he said that she and Adam were welcome to go. The expedition would supply a tent for the Martinez family, he told them, his eyes on Maria's supple hands as the pot grew taller in them.

It made her nervous to have him watch. She felt out of practice because she had been so busy with her garden, housework, and son, that she had little time to do more than replace bowls that had been broken; yet he seemed fascinated by her work. He asked if she sold her pottery. She said that she and the other Pueblo women made only what their families needed and a few for gifts. "What a pity," he murmured, and explained that tourists who visited Santa Fe always wanted to buy good Indian pottery as souvenirs. Maria was embarrassed but pleased that he liked her work.

The group would leave for the mountains in a couple of days, so Maria set the pots outside in the shade to dry. Before they left for the digs, she would bring them into the house to await firing in the fall.

Two days later the same man came to pick up the Martinez family in a large wagon for the trip to the camp. His companion was head of the expedition, Dr. Edgar Lee Hewett, director of the Museum of New Mexico in Santa Fe. Maria remembered that he was the one who had brought Julian home after Yellow Pond Lily's death. Both men asked to see more of Maria's pottery.

She regretted that she had so little to show: just several meal bowls and yeast bowls. While she dressed Adam for the journey, Julian showed the visitors Maria's bowls. She'd used the rough San Ildefonso clay, but she had polished and burnished the pieces until they were as smooth as glass and glossy as a bird's wing.

As they rode out of the pueblo, the men complimented Maria on the pots. Dr. Hewett asked if she ever put designs on them. Maria said that she wasn't good at decorating pottery. Since they were only for household use, why bother? The modest young woman was still amazed at their complimentary remarks about her skills.

It was a wonderful summer for Maria, Julian, and Adam. Three other pueblo women were there with their children, so they kept one another company when the men were at the digs. Each day was peaceful and quiet as the women visited and sat sewing together, watching the children play in the cool mountain air. The troubles of the pueblo seemed far away.

Sometimes it reminded Maria of the happy summer at Little Trees when everything seemed simple and there was not a cloud on the horizon. She explored up and down the mountainsides. One day she found a bed of clay and another time she picked up smooth polishing stones to burnish her pots. She wished she could make pottery, but there would be no place to fire the ware, and raw clay pots were too fragile to survive the trip home.

In one of the caves where the men were digging, they found paintings of water snakes on the walls. Hewett, who had seen Julian sketching one evening, asked him to copy the designs on paper. The drawings the young man made were so fine that the director gave him a fistful of colored pencils and a large pad of drawing paper and encouraged him to fill it with drawings.

Julian did. He drew snakes, costumed dancers, bears, deer, and skunks. That summer Hewett asked Julian to sketch many things. Her husband seemed happiest when he had a colored pencil in his hand, thought Maria, watching an absorbed Julian filling the pad with drawings. Her Julian was an artist forced to be a farmer, she grieved.

As they packed to leave at summer's end, Hewett handed Maria a piece of broken pottery the men had dug up. Could she, he wondered, form a pot that looked like this shard? She examined the piece carefully, noting the designs, and said she would try, but she had never seen any pottery like this. She reminded him that she couldn't draw, so she would be unable to

**FAMOUS INDIAN POTTERY MAKERS    64**

5A-H7773

**JULIAN AND MARIE MARTINEZ**
These famous pottery makers reside at the quaint Indian village of San Ildefonso, which is near Espanola and easily reached from the Santa Fe - Taos Highway.

(over)

*Maria and Julian worked as a pottery making team.*
*On this postcard, Maria goes by the name "Marie".*
*Maria signed her early pots "Marie" because she was*
*told that this name would be better remembered by*
*tourist who visited the museum shops.*

make the designs. He suggested that Julian do the drawings. Maria was doubtful about that idea, since pottery making was woman's work in their tribe. Hewett replied that it seemed natural for them to work together, with Maria forming the pots and Julian decorating them. They could do the work this winter, and next summer when he came back with the expedition, he would buy the pottery.

On the long ride home, Maria thought about what he'd said and kept taking the fragment out of her handkerchief to study it. The small piece was a dark, burnished gray, thin and hard as stone, with a design etched in fine black lines. It was nothing like the pottery she made.

Back at the pueblo, there was much to do. Maria cleaned the house. She stored the harvested corn, beans, squash, and pumpkins in her storeroom. Adam needed new clothes, and Julian's shirts were worn out, as well as most of her dresses, so she spent several weeks at the sewing machine.

During all this work, she thought of the gray pottery shard and how she could replicate it. How did that long-ago potter get it so thin? The walls of the bowls she made were much thicker. Her pottery cracked when it was too thin. Maria puzzled over ways she could make thin-walled vessels.

One sunny day Maria decided it was time to start the pot. She held the shard up to the light and noticed a glitter; then it came to her. The potter must have mixed a very fine sand with the clay to give it strength. Yes, she was pretty sure it was sand, but she decided to ask Tia Nicolasa.

The older woman was also amazed that the shard of pottery was so thin and agreed that the glitter must be fine sand added to strengthen the clay. She told Maria of a place about two hours' distance by wagon where there was a bed of especially fine sand that should be ideal to add to the coarse San Ildefonso clay. She advised Maria to sift the sand to make it even finer and to sift the clay as well before she began her pot. The two women were excited about the possibilities.

Julian and Maria set off sand hunting on a warm December day. When they got to the sand beds, Maria took two flour sacks out of the wagon and filled them. This sand was the finest she'd ever seen, so fine that the little rivulets of it sifted through the new, tightly woven bags.

Maria and Julian enjoyed that day. It was noon when the heavy sacks were hoisted into the wagon, and they ate lunch on the sunny side of a sand dune. As they sat leaning against a wagon wheel, Maria thought about how happy Julian looked. He was a man who liked doing new things; he enjoyed going places and meeting people. Julian was an artist and did not enjoy farming as her father did. Maybe they could make pottery together as Dr. Hewett had suggested.

On the way home, Julian stopped the horses and vaulted out of the wagon near a large yucca. After handing the reins to Maria, he cut the top off the sharp-leafed plant, then tossed it into the wagon. "There," he said. "That ought to make me some good paint brushes." The happy pair could hardly wait to get home to start the new project.

The next morning Maria sifted the sand through a thin piece of worn cloth. It took a long time to fill the large bowl. The clay took even longer to strain since it was so coarse.

Meanwhile, Julian cut a six-inch piece off the yucca. He trimmed the leaves back to the stem until it was a narrow, three-sided stick and chewed the end until it formed a fine, narrow brush. He would use this to decorate the pottery.

Maria mixed the clay and sand with water until it was malleable. She worked the mass until a smooth ball was formed. She knew they could make a pot explode in the firing and blow fragments of clay on the pottery stacked around it, so she did a thorough job.

An excited Maria was ready to start the pot. She broke off a chunk of clay and patted it into a thick, tortilla-shaped base. When it was smooth and flat, she began to twirl coils between her palms. Patiently she rolled coil after coil. The vessel grew. As it took form, she marveled at the strength the sand gave the clay. Now she could make larger pots whose thinner walls would not crack. The fine sand made the difference. Maria was as thrilled as if this were the first pot she had ever made!

Julian watched with pleasure as his wife polished the new, leather-hard bowls that had taken several winter days to dry. As each piece was finished, Maria set it on a table. These were the lightest, best-shaped pots Julian had ever seen. He could hardly wait until they were dry enough to paint designs on their plump and polished sides. His fingers itched to make the first bold stroke.

*Maria formed pots using the traditional technique of coiling clay. She and Julian also gathered clay from the reservation and collected plants to make brushes and dyes.*

Hewett had told Julian that he thought the material used for the designs was guaco (wild spinach), boiled into a thick mixture, then dried, and finally brought back to the thick form by adding water to make a dye. When Nicolasa crossed the plaza to see the new pots, she told Julian she had some of the guaco mixture and he was welcome to use it.

*Julian uses a yucca brush to paint*
*designs on pots as Maria burnishes*
*a pot with a stone.*

When the pottery was finally ready to decorate, Julian gazed at each piece for a long time. He studied their shapes for what Maria thought seemed like hours before he even picked up his yucca brush and dipped it into the guaco. He worked sitting on the floor, each pot placed on a stool before him. His hands were as sure and steady as if he had been decorating pots all his life. Maria loved the designs he drew: a water snake, then some squares to represent the pueblo and the fields around it.

"It looks as if the designs grew on the bowl," Maria said.

"I like this sort of work," Julian replied. "You think about what you're doing, and that makes your hands do it. It's good. Everything goes with you. It's much different from plowing. With plowing, everything goes against you."

In 1909 a new and better life was beginning for the Martinez family. Maria and Julian were becoming partners in pottery making as well as in their marriage. Thanks to this innovative pair, other pueblo men would soon become involved in this ancient craft of their ancestors.

# CHAPTER NINE

Firing her pottery had always been simple for Maria as long as she stacked

the pots carefully, got the fire hot enough, and kept it glowing for the

required time. But firing the decorated pottery was a different story.

She and Tia Nicolasa were not sure how to go about it. They would

have to experiment.

One clear, windless morning, Nicolasa brought over a bunch of her

own pottery. Maria brought her pieces outdoors, and they prepared to fire the ware. Julian dug a shallow hole in the ground behind the house, laid down a bed of cedar bark, and then a layer of broken pottery pieces and scraps of metal. Beside the fire pit, he stacked a pile of wood. They placed Maria's pots on the first layer and then added Nicolasa's. Over the ware, Julian stacked little chunks of wood.

The older woman sprinkled cornmeal over the pile and said a prayer, asking that the finished pottery be beautiful. They piled on more wood and covered the top and sides with cakes of dried cow dung. Now it was time. Julian lit the wood, and the process began.

The fire blazed furiously, hot red flames licking the pots. Every time it began to die, they piled on more wood. If the flames burned unevenly, they placed more sticks where they were needed. After using the large pile of wood, they stopped feeding the fire.

Then, from nowhere, a whirlwind sailed in, and the smoke, which had been rising straight to the sky, whipped down and began swirling around and through the pottery. Maria worried as she watched the smoke curl. Would it smudge her decorated pots, the pots for which she had such great hopes? There was nothing to do but wait and see. The embers must cool enough to remove the pottery.

After a few hours, the three went out to uncover the ware. The pieces should be cool enough, they thought, since the embers were no longer glowing. Nicolasa picked up a long, heavy stick and gently pushed the ashes away from the first layer of  pottery. She thrust the end of the stick into the neck of a jar and carefully inched it out. It looked fine. A few of her pots had fire clouds and smudges, but the others pleased her.

She handed the stick to Maria who gently brought out her own larger pots. They were light and thin and rang clearly in the chilly air as they were handled. After wiping the ashes off, Nicolasa pronounced them perfect.

*Maria and Julian firing pottery.*

Everyone was delighted with Julian's stunning designs on the pots' round sides. But a strange thing happened to two bowls. Rather than being light gray with black designs, they were black all over. What had caused it, they wondered. Strangely enough, these pieces looked like the pottery produced by the women of the Santa Clara pueblo.

Nicolasa suggested that Maria rub lard on them to make the black shine. The young woman did, and although others thought the pots were beautiful, Maria and Julian were disappointed. They set the black pots out of sight in the storeroom. Something strange had happened, and they didn't like the results; in fact, they thought the pots were ugly!

That spring they were far too busy to think of pottery. Tomas and Julian began plowing and getting the fields ready to sow. When that was done, they hoed the weeds, cleaned debris from the irrigation ditches, and planted a garden. It was the season when baby farm animals were born, and there was work to be done with them.

Maria was busy taking care of Adam, her house, and the garden. Every day at noon, she and Reyes took lunch into the fields for the men. Sometimes Julian and Tomas were so tired they had to rest before they could eat. After eating they worked until dark getting the land into shape. It was a busy time for the whole family.

One day there was a knock at the door. Maria was surprised to see Dr. Hewett and his assistant standing there. After visiting for a while, Maria shyly told the men she had made the pottery they asked her to make. She brought out three of the prettiest pieces. They were pleased and praised her for doing such a wonderful job.

When Julian came in from the fields that night, they congratulated him on the striking designs he had drawn on the pots. Everybody discussed prices and agreed that a dollar and a half would be fair for the small pieces and three dollars for the larger ones. Little did they realize that years later these pots would sell for thousands of dollars.

In a short while, Maria had a new baby boy, Juan Diego. Her mother was also pregnant. Reyes was not well, for she was rather old to be giving birth. Her daughters worried about their mother constantly and took turns going up the hill to the big house to help her. Despite all they did, Reyes continued to look worn and tired.

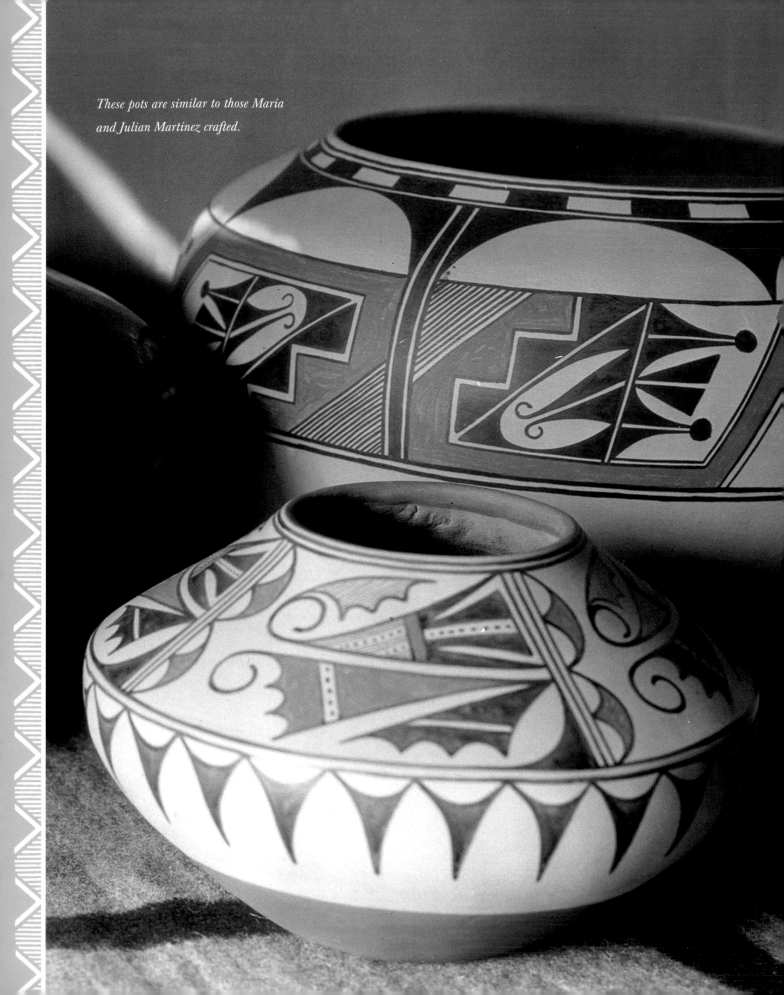

*These pots are similar to those Maria
and Julian Martinez crafted.*

A few weeks after Maria's baby was born, her own frail mother went into a long labor. Finally, after a dark night of struggle, dawn broke, and Clara was born. The dying Reyes lived long enough to see that her daughter was perfect. She asked Maria to take the baby and bring her up with Adam and Juan Diego.

It was a sad and busy time for the young woman, taking care of two babies and her older son, Adam. She grieved sorely for Reyes, because mother and daughter had always been close, but a strong bond was forged between the young woman and her baby sister, for Clara was all she had left of her mother. Ever after, the two sisters remained extremely close. In fact, Clara lived with Maria and Julian all her life, becoming a fine potter herself.

They carried on, but it was a hard winter for the people of San Ildefonso. Money was short, and most of the able-bodied men went to Santa Fe or Albuquerque to work. Some traveled as far as Colorado to seek employment in the sugar beet fields. Once more the women, children, and viejos (old men) were left to rattle around the pueblo.

Just before Julian left for Colorado, Dr. Hewett came to offer him a janitorial job at the museum in Santa Fe. Maria was reluctant to see him go, but he needed a steady paycheck and preferred that to working on a farm somewhere in Colorado. At Hewett's suggestion Julian took some of the 200 pots Maria had made during the summer. He would decorate them at night in his room behind the museum.

During Julian's absence little Adam was his grandfather's devoted companion and helper. He was a dependable child, and young as he was, he took good care of the other children. One day, as Adam was watching the little ones while his mother hoed the garden, Dr. Hewett came. The boy ran to the corn patch to tell his mother that one of the "pottery men" was at the house.

Business had brought Hewett to the pueblo. He explained he came by to pick up more of Maria's pottery for Julian to decorate. He also wished to talk privately with her. He gently told her that Julian seemed sad. Hewett felt that the young man was missing his wife and children, and this was affecting his work.

The museum director said that he had an offer for her. The trustees would furnish an apartment for the Martinez family if Maria and the children would go to live there. The museum gift shop would sell her ware, since visitors to Santa Fe were eager to buy authentic Native American pottery. Julian was a good man, Hewett continued, a steady worker and well liked by all, so they were eager to help the family stay together. Maria knew Julian was a good man. She and the children missed him, but the pueblo was home and she was happiest there. Still, in her culture, a wife's place was with her husband, so she and the children moved to Santa Fe.

Maria enjoyed life at the museum, but she was heartsore for the pueblo, her home, and her family. But there were good things about being in the city. She enjoyed cooking in the convenient kitchen with running water and electric lights, which they didn't have at San Ildefonso. Julian was in his element. The children seemed to be adjusting well to life in Santa Fe, better than she was, she sometimes thought, but she kept busy. Several days a week, she gave Tewa lessons to museum workers who were studying tribal languages, and she made pottery as well.

In the evenings, after the children were settled, she and Julian smoothed and burnished the ware, then Julian applied the designs. They were both practicing their craft so steadily that their creations were growing finer each day. The pots were light, full-bodied, and beautifully shaped. Julian's designs fit them perfectly.

The pair from San Ildefonso were becoming well-known in the Santa Fe art world. The museum gift shop was hard-pressed to keep their pottery in stock. It was so popular with visitors that a shopkeeper on the plaza asked to sell their work as well. The crowds of art-loving tourists could not get enough of Maria's ware, which never ceased to surprise the modest young woman. She did not realize that she and Julian were reviving an art that had very nearly died.

One day, when their stock became depleted, Julian returned to the pueblo to get pieces they had left at home. Since the pottery of Maria's sisters, as well as that of the other women of San Ildefonso, was the same style, Hewett asked him to bring their pots to Santa Fe as well.

Never one to do things by half measure, Julian returned with a wagon load. He had even gone into Maria's storeroom and brought the black pots they had fired before–the ones they considered spoiled. Julian loved to tease, so he told the shopkeeper that the black pots were "special" and should sell for more than the rest of the group!

To their amazement, the next day the shopkeeper came to Julian asking for more black pottery–it seemed the "spoiled" pots were first to sell. Maria threw up her hands when she heard that customers wanted the black pots the smoke had ruined.

"What?" Maria asked. "Well, if the buying public wants black pottery," she reasoned, "black pottery they will get."

Maria and Julian, unsure of how to make the black pottery, decided that maybe they would try to smoke the pieces deliberately during the next firing to see if they achieve the same effect. Maybe they could learn to like the black pots, too.

# CHAPTER TEN

Although Maria learned to enjoy the three years they lived at the museum,

she never stopped longing for the pueblo. It was her home, and she felt safe

and happy there. Julian loved San Ildefonso, but not with the passion Maria

felt. He was more gregarious than she and relished meeting the many

people who came to Santa Fe, already a center of activity for art lovers.

He enjoyed the work at the museum better than farming; there was no

question about that!

It distressed Maria that so many of her people were leaving the pueblo. During the second year they lived in Santa Fe, at the time of the Corn Dance, so few people remained in San Ildefonso that the council sent word to those who were away to come back for the ceremonies. Maria and Julian hurried back to take part in the celebration. Rain or shine, the Corn Dance had always been an event that involved everyone in the pueblo, from toddlers in costume to the oldest adults who danced when they were able.

A bountiful feast was prepared. The men barbecued beef, sheep, goat, or sometimes all three. For days the women worked, making their most special dishes. The long, makeshift tables set up in the plaza were overflowing with delicious food. From dawn the day before to midmorning, loaf after loaf of crusty bread was pulled from the big outdoor ovens to feed the crowds. Its aroma wafted around the plaza and gave the dancers and spectators even greater appetites!

This year the scene was different. Only a few dancers showed up for this special occasion, one of the four most important dance ceremonies held annually at San Ildefonso. The wide plaza looked empty and forlorn with so few Tewas present. The chorus was so small that their singing could barely be heard in the open air.

Maria was depressed. She missed the bustling presence of those who had always returned from near and far. She did not like the lonely, hollow feeling that came over her that day. Although she realized that many of the young people were leaving to find work, she could not understand why they did not come back for this important tribal occasion. The Tewa ways were being lost, and it disturbed and frightened her.

Maria and Julian, mourning the loss of the old ways and shocked at the change in the pueblo, decided they must move back with their children. They were in a predicament though. The crops on Tomas's farm would no

*Maria and Julian never forgot the old ways of their pueblo. Julian is wearing special clothing perhaps to participate in a traditional Tewa ceremony.*

longer support both families. Others who were determined to remain at the pueblo were facing the same problem. How could Tewas make a living and remain in this place they loved, the place their ancestors had established so long ago?

Maria felt that she and Julian should concentrate on making pottery to earn a livelihood. Perhaps they could even retail some of it from their house in the pueblo now that San Ildefonso was visited by people from around the United States, and even Europe. Julian was pretty sure that the museum and storekeeper would continue buying the ware. The couple decided to risk it. If they couldn't manage, they could always return to Santa Fe.

When Julian told Hewett they were leaving, the museum director was sad to see them go, but said he understood that the pueblo was their home. He insisted that they keep sending pottery, especially the blackware. The shopkeeper also put in an order for as many black pots as they could make. Maria continued to puzzle about why the "spoiled" pottery was so popular with pottery collectors.

They returned home. After forming and decorating a load of pots, they prepared to do a firing. They weren't sure how to make the "smoke accident" happen again, but they had a few ideas to try. They knew their livelihood depended on the black pieces.

A few days later, they stacked the pieces on a base of cedar wood and broken pottery shards and heaped wood and dung around them. Maria sprinkled the ritual cornmeal and said her prayer. Julian lit the fire. There was not a breeze stirring, and the smoke did not cover the ware; Julian was afraid the pieces would not be blackened.

Sure enough, when they removed the pots, they were the usual iron-red. There was no black pottery—not until they reached the bottom of the pile. The more deeply buried pots were still red, but they had black

*The popularity of the railroad brought tourists from all over the world to San Ildefonso. Maria and Julian led tours of the pueblo and demonstrated pottery making.*

smudges on the sides. The Martinez team got no solid-black pots out of the firing. Now what would they do?

Julian had always been a whiz at figuring out problems. Even though he was a creative artist, he had a logical mind. The rest of the day he thought about the firing. He poked around the ashes, stared at the pile of wood, and sat holding one of the red pots, studying the black smudges. Finally he seemed to come to some conclusion. Watching from the window where  she sat coiling a large jar, Maria saw him fill a sack with dung from the cattle pen.

Before Maria had a full load of pottery ready for another firing, Julian wished to try an experiment. He thought he knew what made the pots black. As always, Maria trusted her husband's judgment about firing the ware.

The next morning they stacked a few pieces of pottery in the firing pit, and after warning Maria that these might be ruined, Julian built a fire. As soon as the flames were leaping into the air, he went into the shed, brought back a sack, and poured its contents over the blaze. When it hit the flames, a thick cloud of yellow smoke mushroomed above the pit. What was he doing, Maria wondered. He had almost put out the fire! He explained that he wanted to smother the fire partially, but not put it out completely.

After the dung had burned off, the fire blazed up once more. The smoke licked the pots. They continued to load on wood, but no more manure. In time they allowed the fire to die. Now they could only wait for the pots to cool. Would the ware be black?

That night they got little sleep. The hours crept by until the first light when they dressed and went out into the chilly October air to uncover the pottery. As Maria stood clutching her warm shawl around her shoulders, Julian dug into the pit with a heavy forked stick, drew out a pot, and blew off the ashes. It was a deep, gleaming black—more beautiful by far than the accidentally black pots. Each uncovered pot shone. The pots were beautiful, Maria and Julian thought. They did not care for the blackware that had come from the first firing, but these were different. The color was a deep ebony. Julian's experiment worked: by smothering the fire with powered dung and smoking it heavily, they knew it would now be possible to get black pottery in each firing.

Now they were both working steadily at pottery making. Maria was always busy. Her time was spent working at her craft and taking care of her four boys: Adam, Juan Diego, and the two newest babies, Popovi Da and Felipe. Clara was good about helping her with cooking and cleaning, but she was in school in Santa Fe much of the time. Regardless of how much Maria had to do, she still found time to give to those who needed assistance. From helping with newborn babies to caring for the sick and elderly of the pueblo, she was always available to her people. Reyes had set an example that Maria never forgot.

During one of these busy times in 1915, Maria and Julian were again asked to join a group of Native Americans who would demonstrate their dances and pottery at the Panama-California Exposition in San Diego, California. While there, Maria coiled large pots as enthralled crowds stood watching her hands. The fat rolls grew longer as she formed the shapely ware. With daily practice Maria made great strides in her pottery-making skills and began building larger pots to the delight of onlookers.

Dr. Hewett and the exposition workers had built a large Indian village on the fairgrounds for demonstrating Native American culture. This allowed the onlookers to see for themselves what a real pueblo looked like, and it also made the demonstrators feel more at home. Even Maria felt less homesick than she usually did when she was away from the pueblo. Every day she made pottery and danced. When she had time off, she and Julian climbed the hills and walked the beaches of the area, basking in the warm

*At the Panama-California Exposition, Maria demonstrates pottery making with another Native American woman as Julian looks on.*

sun. They were fascinated by the ocean—so different from the dry land of New Mexico. Those few months at the fair were a happy and satisfying time for the couple. With their salaries and the money made from pottery sales, they earned enough to build a store onto their house in the pueblo.

On their return to San Ildefonso, Maria ordered a new stove from the Sears, Roebuck & Company catalog, and they settled back into pueblo life. Before long Maria had a load of pots for a firing. Once again she and Julian would take another giant step in their pottery making.

Julian wanted to try a new design. He took one of Maria's burnished pots and painted a design on it with slip (clay mixed with water to the consistency of thick cream). When this piece came from the fire, it looked different from the rest. It was a burnished black where the piece had been polished and matte black in the area where Julian had painted the design with the slip. They were not sure how well they liked the pot, but it was certainly different from the rest. If customers liked the change, they would make more.

When the Santa Fe storekeeper came to San Ildefonso to pick up more ware, he thought this new batch was especially beautiful. He picked up the pot Julian had decorated with slip and commented on the fact that it was not like the rest of the pieces. Maria, watching his reaction to the new design, noticed that he didn't seem to like or dislike the pots, but he said he'd take them. In time these black-on-black pots became the ware for which Maria was most famous.

Several days later Maria was sitting in the shade wedging clay when two of her friends, Isabel and Tonita, walked into the yard. They wished to talk to Maria about pottery making. They reminded her that they also made pots—pots whose shapes resembled her own. The women were hoping that Maria would ask the storekeeper to buy their pottery regularly, too. Their families were having a hard time since farming was so poor. They were

*An example of one of Maria's*
*black-on-black pots.*

desperate for money, they told her. Some days their children did not have enough to eat.

Listening, Maria recalled the time when Tia Nicolasa was teaching her to make pottery, and how she used to say that people should always share their knowledge. Her aunt had stressed that "pottery making belongs to everyone in the pueblo that wants to make it." Maria also remembered Reyes' unselfish ways and how she had always shared with her neighbors. Maria told Isabel and Tonita that she would gladly ask the storekeeper to buy their work, too.

Her friends also wanted to learn the process of firing that turned the pottery black. In the same spirit of generosity, Maria replied that the next time she and Julian did a firing, the women were welcome to watch. She knew this would be all right with Julian. She and her husband had already talked about their feeling of sadness that others in the pueblo were not having as easy a time as the Martinez family now that they were selling so much pottery. She told her friends to bring their own pots to the first learning session, so they would have something to show for the experience.

Isabel and Tonita went home in a far happier frame of mind. They appreciated Maria's willingness to share and were eager to begin. Soon the other women of the pueblo had enough pieces for a firing. They brought their ware, and Julian taught them how to blacken the pots by controlling the fire and smoke. The next time the shopkeeper came to San Ildefonso, Maria and the other women of the village had many pots waiting for him. He drove away with a wagonload. Would people continue to buy so much pottery, or was it just a passing fancy? If they did, by easing their financial situation, more families could stay in the pueblo instead of looking for employment elsewhere.

*Remembering the words of her Tia Nicolasa, Maria shared her pottery knowledge and helped the women of the pueblo by conducting pottery classes at San Ildefonso.*

WEIGHT—HEIGHT—AGE TABLES
FOR BOYS AND GIRLS

# CHAPTER ELEVEN

By 1930, times were financially better in the pueblo. The pottery of the

other women had also become popular with people, although it was always

Maria's pots they liked best. There was something about her skillful work–

her generous-looking, sturdy, but graceful pots–that were fast becoming

collectors' pieces.

Although Maria and Julian did not originate the black pottery, they

were responsible for making the handsome ware famous. They had blazed the trail, and now art lovers and collectors from around the world came to buy the famed black pottery where it was created. What had been a remote and isolated pueblo was becoming a Native American arts and crafts community.

The years flowed past as relentlessly as the waters of the Rio Grande. Maria's whole life revolved around the pueblo, her husband, the children, and pottery making. Her pieces sold so well that Julian was finally able to quit the farming he hated. Now he devoted most of his time to decorating pottery and painting pictures. He was a talented painter, and his pictures sold well.

Julian bought a fine team of horses to pull the wagon. Maria, whose wants were simple, bought a few things for the house. Soon they were doing so much business in Santa Fe that they needed faster transportation than a horse-drawn wagon, so they purchased the first new automobile to chug into the pueblo. Julian decorated the car in the same manner in which he did Maria's pottery. They attracted much attention as they skittered along the streets of Santa Fe in this vehicle. People always knew when the Martinez family came to town, for there was no other automobile covered with hand-painted designs.

Though they still sold their work in Santa Fe shops and museums, they retailed much of it from the combination workroom and trading post they had added to their home with their earnings from one of the world's fairs. Julian worked at his paintings and pottery, keeping to the front room where people could see him. Customers enjoyed watching him decorate the ware. They were fascinated by the precise way he drew the designs with his homemade yucca brushes. His work was so perfect, they were amazed that he didn't draw from a pattern. The lines girdling the pots were so straight that it was hard to believe he did not use a ruler.

Those who bought told others, and orders streamed in. Before long they were taking loads of pottery into Santa Fe by truck for mailing all over the world. As it became fashionable to have a "Maria pot," buyers asked her to sign her name on the bottom of each piece so it could be identified as her work.

During this time Maria often thought that although people of the pueblo had more money, in some ways things were not as good as they had been in the old days. Maria mourned the loss of many Tewa traditions and regretted that many young people were giving up their "Indian ways." Cars were becoming more popular, and a gas station was built just outside the pueblo. It seemed to Maria that "people spent more time running up and down the roads than they did in the pueblo."

The Martinez sons grew up. Adam was a good deal older than the other three sons, and sometimes it seemed to Maria that her father's spirit dwelt in him. He loved the pueblo, its traditions, and dances, and was a good farmer like Tomas. Adam married a Tewa girl, and they moved into the family home. Much of the time when his father was gone, Adam became the man of the house and was Maria's greatest comfort.

Juan Diego, the Martinezes' second son, who was born in 1909, did not have the interest in pottery making that his brothers did. From day one, the little boy had his nose buried in a book. He loved school and made high marks. Juan Diego attended school in Santa Fe, where he became interested in sports. He became a good athlete, and after attending military school in Georgia, his teachers urged the young man to go to college. They foresaw a brilliant future for him. He studied engineering at Stanford University in California and played on the varsity football team.

Popovi Da (Red Fox), their third son, born in 1923, was a talented potter. Po belonged to a new generation of Native American men who now painted and made pottery. Thanks to Julian and Dr. Edgar Hewett, many San Ildefonso men were becoming pottery makers.

*Maria holding a black-on-black plate. Her mastery of pottery and innovative techniques led to the acceptance of pottery as an art form.*

One of the most important and loved members of the household was Maria's youngest sister, Clara, who had lived with the Martinez family since the death of the girls' mother shortly after Clara's birth.

The little girl went to school in Santa Fe as Maria had done. She was intelligent, studied hard, and was eager to please her teachers. Everything seemed to be going well until she was about 12 years old. That winter Clara caught a terrible cold, which seemed to settle in her ears. The infection left her hearing impaired, and she returned home to San Ildefonso. She became Maria's little shadow, doing whatever her sister did.

Maria always said that Clara lived in a quiet world of her own. The younger sister was a happy person, quiet and modest. Although she became a fine potter, she never sought attention, preferring to be Maria's helper.

Since she had always lived in this household where pottery work was a large concern, Clara shouldered responsibility early and was Maria and Julian's "right hand." When it came to firing, glazing, or any of the other steps in pottery making, Clara was there to take up the slack. She often traveled with the family, but other times she preferred to stay in the pueblo, caring for the younger boys and visiting with her older sisters.

Maria and Julian continued pottery demonstrations at world's fairs and exhibitions. They went to the New York State Fair in 1925 and to the Chicago World's Fair in 1934. The San Francisco World's Fair of 1939 was the last in which Maria and Julian demonstrated. Those were always good times for the couple. They took the boys and Clara with them when they could. The family enjoyed sightseeing and climbed to the tops of skyscrapers, clambered aboard subways, and always talked to people they met.

In 1934, along with eight other Native American artists, Maria and Julian worked at a tribal exposition in Alabama and, from there, continued to Washington, D.C. The artists traveled together by government cars. In the early evening or early morning when they stopped, Julian left their

*Maria and Julian demonstrating their pottery making skills in Washington, D.C.*

lodgings with a small sack and walked into the countryside to find clay. He dug enough from the states between New Mexico and the capital for Maria to form a pot from each state.

When they arrived in Washington, President Franklin D. Roosevelt[5] was out of the country on a state visit, but they met his wife, Eleanor.[6] They were surprised at what a friendly and down-to-earth First Lady she was. The gracious woman told them that Native American art was important to all Americans. She urged them to teach their craft to coming generations so these priceless treasures would not be lost.

[5] **Franklin D. Roosevelt (1882-1945)**. The 32nd president of the United States, Franklin Delano Roosevelt was the first president to address the nation over the radio.

[6] **Eleanor Roosevelt (1884-1962)**. Wife of President Franklin D. Roosevelt, she was an inspiration to other women of her time. Eleanor Roosevelt was active as a lecturer and newspaper columnist.

As always, Maria and Julian managed to squeeze in some sightseeing during the six days they were in the city. They made a striking couple, even in Washington, a place that was home to distinguished people and foreign diplomats. In their bright tribal clothes of rich velvet and buckskin, and soft, knee-high moccasins, their arms and necks loaded with heavy silver and turquoise jewelry, and their glossy black hair bound back from their faces, they stopped traffic wherever they went. Unintentionally, they made wonderful ambassadors of the Native American nations.

By now Maria's work was well-known, and she had grown more comfortable with strangers. She was so sure of her pottery skills that she didn't even mind people watching her work. Still, getting home to San Ildefonso was always a tremendous relief. Her roots were deep and strong in the northern New Mexico soil. This country of cedar- and piñon-covered hills beneath a wide blue sky was in her very soul. When she had been away, Maria always looked forward to the first sight of Black Mesa. When she saw it, she knew she was safely home.

Back at the pueblo, Maria formed a series of state pots. Julian decorated each one symbolically. For instance, on the Texas pot, he drew a lone star; for Oklahoma, he sketched a feather, and on a pot for Washington, D.C., he placed a winding river.

During that time, a neighbor asked Maria what state she liked the best while they were traveling. Ever the potter, Maria answered promptly, "Tennessee. It has the best clay."

Julian had no art training, but he was an accomplished Native American painter. Some of his paintings of Native American life are on display at the Smithsonian American Art Museum in Washington, D.C.

# CHAPTER TWELVE

In 1940, Julian was elected governor of the pueblo, an honor given to the

most important man in the village. The one chosen was in charge of the

council that took care of all pueblo business, but he was head of the

religious life as well. To be governor was the greatest honor a pueblo

man could receive.

Since he was a sensitive person, Julian was extremely conscious of his

responsibility and was proud to be honored in this way. He was respected by his people; they knew him to be a kind and upright man who was fair and had the good of the pueblo at heart. Julian was always willing to stand up and speak out for what he believed.

Back in Civil War times, President Abraham Lincoln had given all pueblo governors gold-headed canes as symbols of office. Now the San Ildefonso cane passed to Julian, who hung it on the front wall of the pottery store for all to enjoy.

It was a difficult time to be governor. World War II was threatening, and it seemed as if the United States must join the Allies in their fight against Germany, Japan, and Italy. Men of the nation were subject to the draft and could be called into the armed services at any time. Many young men did not wait to be drafted, but volunteered for duty before their call. This was especially worrisome for Julian, since he and Maria had four sons who could be called upon to fight.

Sure enough, Felipe, their youngest, who was underage, was one of the first young men in the pueblo to volunteer to serve the nation. Sadly, his father gave the lad his permission to join the Navy. He was proud of his son's patriotism, but he and Maria grieved that he was going.

Julian governed the pueblo well during that time, but his health was poor. One snowy winter day in 1943, Maria realized that the house was far too quiet. Julian usually whistled softly as he painted his canvases or decorated his pottery. She hurried into the salesroom, but he was not there or anywhere in the house. Maria went to the back door and called several times, thinking he might be at the barn, but she received no answer. She asked Adam to look for him, for it was freezing outside–too cold to be wandering around outdoors. The older man could not be found. Finally the men of the pueblo mounted a search for him.

Maria slept little during the next four nights while they searched for her husband. The men hurried to places where Julian usually went. They asked everyone within miles if they had seen him, but no one had. Maria was too sad for tears, but her heart ached for the man she had loved for so many years. Where could he be?

That fourth night Maria finally fell into a deep sleep and did not awaken until dawn when she heard voices outside her window. In a moment Adam came into her bedroom. As soon as she saw his face, she knew the news was bad. Julian was dead. He had been found lying at the top of a snow-covered hill.

After the funeral the men of the pueblo, following Tewa custom, took Julian's body away. Maria would never know where they had taken him, and in the Tewa tradition, they took his clothes, paints, and brushes, too. The things he had used in his life must go with him in his next one.

After the men returned, the family had a feast for the pueblo to celebrate Julian's life and to comfort Maria. They ate and talked about the absent one and told stories of things he had done and said. Part of the time they wept, and then they remembered how Julian loved a joke and that made them laugh.

For four years after her husband's death, Maria grieved so deeply that she made no pottery. When she resumed her work, her ware was more in demand than ever. Now Santana, Adam's wife, decorated Maria's wares. The younger woman utilized some of Julian's designs, but she created new ones of her own, as well.

As the years passed, Popovi Da also helped Maria with the firing and decoration of her pots. Popovi was a confident man. People respected him as a religious and ceremonial leader, and like his father before him, Po served as governor of San Ildefonso. But there was an important added ingredient to his personality; he was as comfortable in the Anglo artistic world as he was in his own pueblo. He was a great speaker and welcomed every chance to inform and educate the public about Native American pottery traditions. As a result he exerted a great deal of influence on the Pueblo pottery industry. He encouraged and gave fellow Native Americans the confidence to enter arts and crafts shows across the Southwest, venues they had been too timid to try before. In his own work, Po held to the lofty standards of his parents and expected his fellow artists to do the same. Although he was grounded in traditional methods, he evolved better ways of firing and glazing the ware. He was the first contemporary Pueblo potter to add turquoise to his pots.

*In 1966, Maria and her son Popovi Da demonstrated pottery making on television. Popovi formed the clay as Maria looked on.*

It has been said that in this stage of Maria's life, if Popovi Da had not been working with her, she probably would have retired. Forming pots was becoming more difficult for her—the strength of her hands and arms was not what it once was. Her pots were not as light and thin-walled as they had been, but they were still full-bellied. If one of her pots was not quite symmetrical, Po would lovingly straighten the piece before it began to dry. Many critics feel this period "expressed the highest level of Maria's genius."

Even as an elderly woman, Maria continued to travel and receive honors–her place in the art world demanded it. Maria made several more trips to the White House. She was invited during the presidency of Herbert Hoover and honored again by presidents Dwight Eisenhower[7] and Lyndon Johnson.[8] She formed a friendship with Joan Mondale, the wife of Walter Fritz Mondale, who was vice president when Jimmy Carter[9] was president. Mrs. Mondale was also a potter and had a deep appreciation of Maria's skilled craft.

Mrs. Mondale visited Maria in San Ildefonso. Maria was one of the potters she admired the most, and she wished to see how and where her pots were made. The younger woman was charmed by the ever-gracious Maria, who usually enjoyed visitors and was generous with her time.

One day, while the vice president's wife was visiting the pueblo, she admired a particularly graceful piece of pottery. Maria simply picked up a nail off the work table, scratched her name on the bottom of the piece, and gave it to Mrs. Mondale. It has been said that the last pot Maria made was for her.

Mrs. Mondale wasn't Maria's first distinguished visitor. Maria had drawn many notable people to the quiet pueblo of San Ildefonso. In 1952, two internationally famous potters from Japan, Shoji Hamada and Sōetsu Yanagi made pilgrimages to San Ildefonso to see Maria and witness one of her firings.

The day they arrived, Maria was outside, ready to uncover her

[7] Dwight Eisenhower (1890-1969). U.S. Army general and the 34th president, Eisenhower was active in the civil-rights movement.
[8] Lyndon Johnson (1908-1973). Vice president to John F. Kennedy, Johnson became the 36th president after Kennedy was assassinated. He saw a major Civil Rights Act through Congress.
[9] Jimmy Carter (1924-    ). The 39th president of the U.S., Carter was successful in negotiating a peace treaty between Egypt and Israel.

cooling pots after a firing. The visitors knocked, received no answer, and knowing the way of potters, went around the house to the backyard. Laura Gilpin, Maria's friend, had accompanied them to the pueblo. She introduced the two men, who were fascinated by Maria's casual way of hooking a pot out of the pile with a hefty stick she had picked up from the ground. Both Japanese potters were impressed with the beauty and simplicity of the pieces they saw that day. These three potters, with different styles and traditions, who were the best of their kind in the ceramic world, felt completely at home with one another, regardless of language difficulties.

Throughout her elderly years, Maria continued to share the way of her craft with others. When she was over 90 years old, with Clara, Adam, Santana, and her great-granddaughter, Barbara Gonzales, Maria went to the University of Southern California's summer pottery session at the Idlewild School of the Arts to demonstrate her ceramic skills. In the evenings, there in the mountains, Adam played his rawhide drum, and the family danced. Maria, seated by the fire, would thrust up her chin, tap her moccasin-booted foot, and chant the words of songs in a high, wailing voice. It was a spellbinding time for the students!

Several colleges awarded Maria honorary degrees. Maria, who loved to joke, said, "When my son tells me that the University of Colorado wants to give me a doctorate, I say, 'Tell these men I don't want to be a doctor! I never medicate anyone!'" But she did go to Boulder in 1953 to receive the honorary degree and bronze medal for outstanding artistic achievement. She had always loved pretty clothes, so she wore a cap and gown for a part of the ceremony, but in the end she removed the academic robe, keeping the cap on, so that everyone could see her beautiful dress.

In 1968 she went to Los Angeles to accept the American Ceramic Society's highest award for lifelong dedication to pottery. She loved the City of Angels and went sightseeing every day she was there.

Some of the most knowledgeable art collectors in the world bought Maria's work, including Nelson Rockefeller.[10] Those who came to San Ildefonso found her still forming small pots at the age of 91, surrounded by children, grandchildren, and great-grandchildren, all making pottery. One day she said to her great-granddaughter Barbara, "When I am gone, essentially other people have my pots. But to you I leave my greatest achievement, which is the ability to do it."

After being in frail health for several years, on the night of July 20, 1980, Maria died. Her years as a potter had numbered over 70. Many had named her the "most famous Native American artist in history." Maria had almost single-handedly brought about a pottery renaissance, reviving a dying art, which she unselfishly shared with her fellow potters.

Prayers were said for her soul and eulogies were given in many countries. President Carter and Vice President Mondale sent condolences, and newspapers worldwide carried word of the great lady's passing. But the people of San Ildefonso mourned most deeply. Their matriarch was dead. Nobody had ever done so much for the pueblo and its people.

Maria Martinez was a modest woman bursting with creative energy, yet she was warm and human. Her noble spirit, generosity, sense of humor, fertile mind, and skilled hands enriched the world of art. Wife, mother, and potter, she did not regard herself as anything special. In life, Maria passed her skill on to her children and grandchildren. Today many of her descendants still live in San Ildefonso, and they, too, are recognized as great potters. Like their matriarch, they will pass the tradition of Tewa pottery making on to their own children. Through them, Maria's work will live on.

[10] **Nelson Rockefeller (1908–1979).** Nelson Aldrich Rockefeller was vice president of the United States from 1974 to 1977, when Gerald Ford was president. The Rockefeller family fortune began with the Standard Oil Company, and the family is famous for its participation in American business, philanthropy (charity), and politics for nearly a century.

*Portait of Maria Martinez*

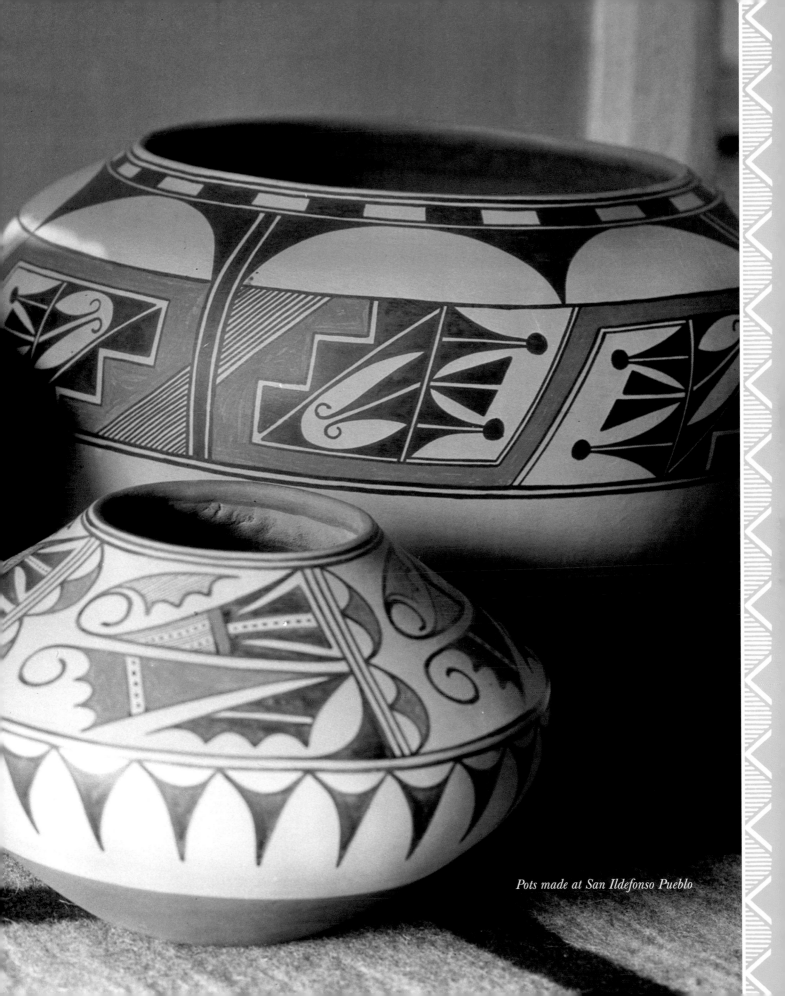

*Pots made at San Ildefonso Pueblo*

# MUSEUMS THAT SHOW
# MARIA'S POTTERY

Andrea Fisher Fine Pottery, **Santa Fe, New Mexico**

Cincinnati Art Museum, **Cincinnati, Ohio**

Mark Sublette Medicine Man Gallery, **Tucson, Arizona and Santa Fe, New Mexico**

Museum of Indian Arts/Laboratory of Anthropology, **Santa Fe, New Mexico**

National Museum of the American Indian, **New York, New York**

Nedra Matteucci Galleries, **Santa Fe, New Mexico**

Panhandle-Plains Historical Museum, **Canyon, Texas**

Smithsonian Institution, **Washington, D.C.**

Southwestern Museum of the American Indian, **Los Angeles, California**

The Millicent Rogers Museum, **Taos, New Mexico**

Wichita Art Museum, **Wichita, Kansas**

# GLOSSARY

ACEQUIA (uh-SAY-kee-a) ditches that carry water from rivers and streams to irrigate crops.

ADOBE (uh-DOE-be) buildings and homes made of sun-dried mud clay bricks. The walls of adobe houses are cool in the summer and warm in the winter.

ARROYO (uh-ROY-oh) a gulley on the desert floor. Arroyos are dry most of the year but turn into floodways during heavy rains.

CARDING WOOL short pieces of wool combed and cleaned with a sharp-toothed instrument and ready to be spun and woven.

CASITA (kuh-SEE-ta) little house (from *casa*, Spanish for "house").

FIRE to use extreme heat to bake or dry pottery.

KILN an oven for burning, baking, or drying pottery.

MANO (MAH-no) the smooth stone that fits into the groove in a metate, where it is pushed back and forth to grind corn or other grain.

METATE (meh-TAH-tay) a large stone with a groove in its top where corn or other grain is ground using a mano.

OLLA (OY-uh) a large clay pot or jar used for storing flour, corn, or other grain.

PILGRIMAGE a journey to a religious shrine for the purpose of showing faith or for healing. The person making the journey is called a pilgrim.

PUEBLO one of many Native American villages in Southwestern United States consisting of flat-roofed stone or adobe houses joined in groups, sometimes several stories high.

PUKI a small bowl-shaped dish used to form and support the base of a pot as the clay is being formed.

RABBITBRUSH a shrub with clusters of yellow or white flowers found in western North America.

RENAISSANCE (REN-uh-sahns) French, meaning "rebirth."

ROSARIO Spanish for "rosary."

SHARDS pieces of broken pottery; usually refers to those found at archaeological dig sites.

SMALLPOX an often fatal disease causing high fever and a severe skin rash.

SLIP clay mixed with water to the consistency of thick cream.

TAMALE (Tah-MAHL-eh) a traditional Mexican food made of cornmeal and chilies and, commonly, a meat filling, wrapped in a corn husk and cooked by steaming or frying.

TIA (TEE-uh) Spanish for "aunt."

VESSEL a container, such as a bowl or jar, meant to hold liquid.

WEDGE process used to work out air bubbles in clay.

YUCCA (YUK-uh) one of several varieties of North American desert plants with a base of long, rigid leaves and a cluster of white flowers on a long, thick stem. The leaves have tough fibers that can be separated and used as a paintbrush.

W. Langdon Kihn 38